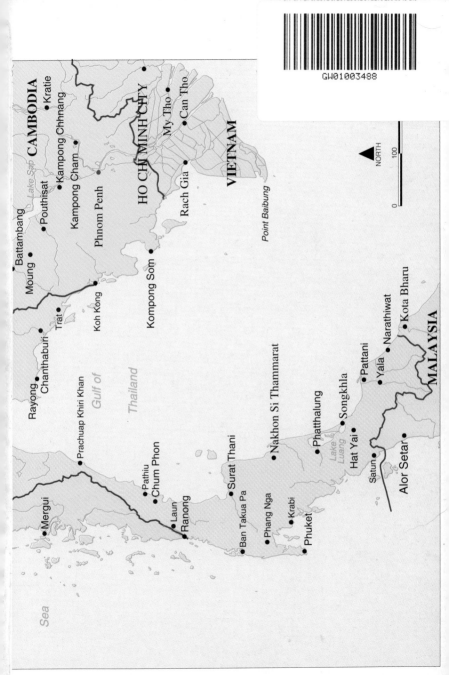

Thailand

Thailand

David Bowden

Little Hills Press

Publisher
Little Hills Press Pty Ltd
Regent House, 37-43 Alexander Street
Crows Nest, NSW, 2065, Australia

ISBN 1 86315 118 4

email: info@littlehills.com
Home Page: http://www.littlehills.com

DISCLAIMER

Whilst all care has been taken by the editorial team to ensure that
the information is accurate and up to date, the publishers do not
take responsibility for the information published herein. As things
get better or worse, places close and others open, some elements in
the book may be inaccurate when you get there. **Please write and
tell us about it so we can update in subsequent editions. We will
give you a free book for your trouble.**

Contents

About the Author

For the past 10 years, David Bowden has travelled extensively throughout Asia. David was born in Australia and has spent the last few years living and working in South-East Asia. His original desire to visit the region began as an undergraduate of geography at the University of Newcastle, NSW. After teaching about the region he decided it was time to head off and discover many destinations that had been merely names in text books.

David eventually turned these trips into working holidays while employed by an adventure travel company operating from Australia. He first accompanied groups to Thailand in 1985 and since then has visited the country many times. His trusty battered collection of Canon cameras and lenses were never too far away to record these destinations. Many of his photographs have been used and published throughout the world. He has also written several text books, children's reading books, articles for magazines and newspapers as well as the Little Hills Press guide to *Cambodia*.

His keen interest in the environment has lead to a career in environmental education in Australia, Malaysia and Cambodia.

This book is dedicated to those travellers who respect the customs of their Thai hosts and the environment in which they live. It is also written as a guide to assist travellers discover, explore and meet their Thai hosts. This guide will aid that process but it will not replace good old fashioned communications between people willing to learn from each other. It is also written for fellow travellers who have made these journeys through the region so rewarding. Special thanks go to all those who have contributed to this book: Chattan Kunjara Na Ayudhya (TAT, Bangkok), Premsiri Devahastin (Thailand), Oithip Nitiyanant (TAT, Bangkok), Loh Lo Mei (Malaysia), Christine Woo (Thailand), Maria Teh (Malaysia), Wisoot Bauchoom (TAT, Chiang Mai), Prasert Changlek (Thailand) & Thaworn Maisupa (Thailand).

Preface

All prices in this book are in either the local currency, *baht* (pronounced *bart*), or in $US. The baht, at the time of writing was B26 to $US1. Metric figures have been used with 1km being equal to 0.6 miles. The spelling for Thai names that have been translated into English varies according to the phonetic pronunciation. This means the same name may be written differently throughout the country or in other books. Neighbouring Myanmar is not referred to as Burma. Myanmar is the name given to the country by the military-backed *Slorc* government. It is probably politically correct to refer to the old name of Burma, but Myanmar it is, as this is the official name. What was once known as Laos is referred to as Lao PDR (Peoples' Democratic Republic); the current official name. Cambodia ceased to be called Kampuchea some years back.

One thing is certain, nothing in the travel industry stays constant. Prices go up, new hotels are built and restaurants change ownership. The information in this guide is as accurate as it could be when it was written. One problem in compiling this guide was the variation in phone numbers listed with different organisations. Many have been checked for their accuracy but some will have changed. By the time you read this guide, most information will be the same, but some small changes will have occurred.

The book should be used as a guide; after all, it is a **guide** book. To ensure the next edition remains accurate, please send all changes and additions to the publisher.

Abbreviations

AIDS	Acquired Immune Deficiency Syndrome
APEC	Asia-Pacific Economic Co-operation
ASEAN	Association of South East Asian Nations
GDP	Gross Domestic Product
GMT	Greenwich Mean Time
GNP	Gross National Product
HIV	Human Immunodeficiency Virus
IDD	International Direct Dialling

ISO	Film is rated according to it's ISO, or film speed
IUCN	International Union for Conservation of Nature and Natural Resources (or World Conservation Union)
Lao PDR	The correct term for Laos. PDR stands for Peoples' Democratic Republic
NIC	Newly-industrialised country
NGO	Non-Government Organisation
SLORC	State Law and Order Restoration Committee, the name taken by the Myanmar (Burmese) government
SEA	South East Asia
TAT	Tourism Authority of Thailand
UN	United Nations
UNESCO	United Nations Educational, Scientific & Cultural Organisation
USA	United States of America
WHO	World Health Organisation
WMO	World Meteorological Organisation

Photographs

David Bowden retains the copyright for all photographs in this book. Enquiries regarding the use of these should be directed to:

The Picture Library
120M Jalan SS21/35
Damansara Utama
47400 Petaling Jaya
Malaysia
Ph/Fax 60 3 7324603
email: tehml@pc.jaring.my

Thailand

Located in South-East Asia, the Kingdom of Thailand is bordered by Myanmar to the west and north, Lao PDR to the north-east, Cambodia to the west and Malaysia to the south.

As a tourist destination, Thailand offers many different natural landscapes, depth of culture and adventure as well as relaxation. The food and shopping are good and make Thailand a value-for-money destination. Tourism is big business in Thailand and is growing every year. In 1996, an estimated 6.5 million visited the country. Revenue from tourism is about $6 billion. Many tourists are repeat visitors; in 1993, 46% of people entering the Kingdom were doing so for at least the second time. Thailand is becoming a base for holidays into the nearby countries of Lao PDR, Myanmar, Cambodia and Vietnam.

Rapid economic growth is bringing about many changes in Thailand. While the quality of living is rising for most, there have been some concerns that this has occurred with costs to the environment and traditional ways of life.

Geography

The country is 513,115km^2 in area, and measures about 1850km from the far north of the country to the southern extremities around Narathiwat and the Malaysian border. Central Thailand is about 550km wide east to west, but around Prachuap Khiri Khan, south of Hua Hin, the Myanmar border is only about 30km from the Gulf of Thailand. The Andaman Sea borders the western coastline of southern Thailand and is 870km long. The Gulf of Thailand coastline, which forms part of the Sunda Shelf, is 1850km long, but the waters here only average 30m in depth. Water temperatures average 26°-28°C and are therefore very tempting for year round watersports. The country lies between latitudes 6°N and 20°N, and longitudes 97°E and 106°E.

Thailand is divided into five distinct regions: the *mountainous north* where it is still possible to see elephants working in the forests and where lower temperatures enable the cultivation of temperate crops; the sprawling *north-east plateau* bordering the Mekong River (the 4425km long river known in Thai as the 'mother of waters') and where the world's oldest Bronze Age civilisation flourished 5600 years ago; the *central plain*, one of world's most fertile rice growing areas fed by the Chao Phraya River; the *eastern coastal plain* where many famous, and some still to be discovered, beaches are located; and the *peninsular south* with its diverse scenery, rubber cultivation and coastal fishing.

History

Archaeological discoveries near the north-east hamlet of Ban Chiang suggest that the Isan culture, a Bronze Age civilisation, existed in north-east Thailand 5600 years ago.

Successive waves of immigrants, including Mons, Khmers and Thais, gradually entered the area now known as Thailand. Most followed the fertile valleys leading from China. By the 11th and 12th centuries, the Khmer civilisation, centred on Angkor (in modern day Cambodia), ruled much of the region.

By the early 13th century, Thais had established small northern city states in Lanna, Phayao and Sukhothai. In 1238, two Thai chiefs rebelled against Khmer rule and established the first truly independent Thai Kingdom in Sukhothai. During the Sukhothai period Thai dominance gradually expanded throughout the entire Chao Phraya River basin, and Theravada Buddhism was introduced as the paramount religion. Also, the Thai alphabet and the first expression of Thai art forms, including painting, sculpture, architecture and literature, became identifiable.

In the 1300s, Sukhothai's regional dominance declined. It eventually became a vassal state of Ayutthaya, the new kingdom further south, near the mouth of the Chao Phraya River. Founded in 350AD, Ayutthaya remained the capital until 1767 when it was destroyed by Burmese invaders.

During Ayutthaya's 417 years as the capital, under the rule of 33 kings, the distinct Thai culture evolved. In so doing, they drove out the Khmers (Cambodians) and fostered contact with Arabian, Chinese, Indian, Japanese and European powers (particularly Portugal which then controlled Malacca in present day Malaysia). The Khmers had exerted a strong influence over the Thai people.

The previous Thai kings had been father-like figures who guided their people, but during the Ayutthaya period they became more god-like, similar to those in Khmer society.

Ayutthaya's destruction was a severe blow to the Thais. However, a revival soon occurred and within a few months the Burmese were expelled by King Taskin who later made Thon Buri his capital (it was located on the western banks of the Chao Phraya River in present day Bangkok). In 1782, the first king of the present Chakri dynasty, Rama 1, established his new capital on the site of a riverside hamlet called Ban Kok ('Village of the Wild Plums'). In 1892 a Western-styled council of ministers was established under the Radical Reorganisation. Under this program, with a monarchy lead by King Chulalongkorn, Siam managed to avoid European colonialism.

Thailand is unique in the region in that it has never been colonised by a European power. In 1932, absolute monarchy was replaced with constitutional monarchy and in 1939, the name of the country was changed from Siam to Thailand.

When Thailand became threatened at the outbreak of World War II, it allowed Japanese forces passage through the country. In so doing, war was declared on Britain and the USA although, in the case of the latter, the declaration was never actually delivered to the Americans.

In the 1960s Thailand was staunchly anti-communist and the USA war machine in Indochina established bases throughout Thailand. The Thai government has also maintained realistic relationships with other leading powers like China and the former USSR. Thai soldiers fought in the Korean and Vietnamese conflicts. For many years the military has controlled the country with coups d'etats being common (there have been almost 20 under the current King's reign). The most celebrated of these was in mid-May 1992 when hundreds of civilians were shot on the streets while protesting the election to Prime Minister of military strongman, General Suchinda.

In this incident, the King stepped in and negotiated a settlement which ultimately pardoned the military for the killings. However, constitutional change was implemented and more capitalist-oriented governments emerged in the 1990s.

Government

Thailand is a constitutional monarchy with a democratic government. Up until 1932, the country had an absolute monarchy but then the first constitution was implemented. The Head of State is the King; currently King Bhumiphol Adulyadej (King Rama IX). His wife is Queen Sirikit. The King appoints the Prime Minister on the advice of the elected National Assembly. The government is run by a Council of Ministers. The bicameral parliament consists of a Senate whose members are appointed by the King on the Prime Minister's recommendation, and an elected House of Representatives.

King Bhumiphol has been king since 1946. Celebrations were held in 1995 and 1996 for the 50th anniversary (golden jubilee) of his accession. Celebrations on 6.6.96 marked the longest reigning monarch in the world today. He and his queen are greatly revered by his people. He is well liked for his hands-on approach to solving many of the country's problems.

The nation views itself as being built upon three foundations represented in the red, white and blue of the nation's flag (there are five horizontal bands of red, white, dark blue, white and red, in the flag). The purity of religion is the white in the flag, the land and its people are the red, and the monarchy, which binds the other two elements together, is the blue.

There are 73 provinces each administered by a governor. A province is divided into districts, clusters of settlements and villages. In Thai, these are known as *amphoe, tambons* and *muu baan*. The capital of each province is known as *amphoe muang*.

Since World War II, the army has controlled the government for all but a few brief periods of civilian rule. Increasingly, civilian politicians are challenging the political dominance of the military in seeking greater democracy. A more liberal political system is emerging as Thailand becomes a strong international economy. The political incident of May 1992 appears to have brought the middle class and business interests centre stage at the expense of the conservative military.

The judicial powers are handled by the law courts. Changes to the constitution are common with 15 new charters added since its inception. The most recent changes were implemented in February 1995. The constitution is seen as an ideal that the country should strive to reach. In reality, some sections are not implemented and the government aims to rectify laws that are in contradiction to the constitution.

The King exercises his legislative powers through a National Assembly. Executive powers are controlled through a 49-member Cabinet, headed by a Prime Minister, currently Chavalit Yongchaiyudh. Several Prime Ministers back, Chuan Leekpai, was the longest serving Thai Prime Minister although he was only in power for two and a half years.

Recently the legal voting age was reduced from 20 to 18 in time for the 2.6.95 elections. Elections in November 1996 saw the New Aspiration Party headed by Chavalit sweep into power. Although 50.04% of the population are women, their presence constitutes only 6.1% of the House of Representatives. The constitution calls for one elected member per 150,000 voters or 391 seats. During elections, accusations of gerrymandering, vote buying, bribes and sinister plots are usually made.

While governments come and go, the bureaucracy remains stable and it is here that many decisions are made. Policies are determined in Bangkok and radiate down to the smallest village. At the local level though, there is little central control. The governor of each province is also very powerful and influential.

In the early 1990s, approximately 50% of elected politicians at all levels were well-known business people.

The former Indochinese countries are high on the business and policy agendas of both Thai government and corporate leaders. Investments in all three Indochinese countries (Lao PDR, Vietnam and Cambodia) are high.

Political ties with their neighbours have not always been good. Thailand considered its national security threatened when Cambodia was occupied by the Vietnamese communists in 1978. Certain elements in Thailand are still accused of supporting the Khmer Rouge in Cambodia despite official government denials. Relationships with Myanmar (both with the SLORC government and some Myanmar guerilla groups fighting the government) are somewhat strained although there seems to be some recent softening of this attitude. Thailand supports the ASEAN view of constructive engagement with Myanmar. Thailand is an integral member of ASEAN. This policy advocates change through persuasion rather than aggressive diplomacy. However, Thailand's patience is tested when fleeing guerilla groups seek political asylum in the country.

Economy

Until recently, Thailand was one of the poorest economies in the world. Today, it is one of the fastest growing in South-East Asia. This turn around was initiated under a series of five-year plans and is often referred to as an economic miracle. Recent export figures are $43.5 billion per year. The country consistently reports growth rates of between 7% to 8% per annum. Economists and geographers refer to Thailand as many things, namely, developing and a newly industrialised country (NIC). The wealth exhibited in some parts of Thailand would suggest Thailand is far from 'developing', however, visitors to Thailand need to appreciate the big economic discrepancy between urban and rural populations. The per capita GDP for 1994 was $2348 but inflation of 5.1% per annum cuts into the real spending powers of Thais.

Many of the farmers living on the rich fertile plains of central Thailand are only leaseholders. Ownership of land is a contentious issue for these people and other farmers in the country. During periods of hardship many farmers are forced to mortgage their land and crops to money-lenders who charge prohibitive interest rates. In many ways this is holding back the economic growth of the agricultural sector.

The promotion of foreign investment is central to the government's economic policies. While most people are employed in agriculture, its contribution to GDP is small, only about 12%, while manufacturing contributes 27%. Many foreign companies use cheap labour in Thailand for manufacturing products for export (the minimum daily wage in 1993 was $5/day). The 1994 GNP per capita of $2348 compares with a regional GDP average of $684. GDP growth is 7.4% per annum.

Foreign investment principally comes from Japan, Hong Kong, Taiwan and Singapore. Thai companies are expanding regionally particularly into neighbouring Indochina. Business is mostly controlled by families of Chinese and Sino-Chinese origins; maybe as few as 100 to 150 families.

The Bangkok Stock Exchange is one way in which investors

can invest in the economic growth of the country. Valued at $150 billion it is one of the largest in the region.

In 1991, rubber production, mainly in the southern Thailand, surpassed that of Malaysia, up until then the world's largest producer. Exports in the rubber industry grew by a massive 33% in 1993 to 1994.

Climate

The climate is tropical with long hours of sunshine and high temperatures. The mountainous areas in the north are slightly cooler. The average temperature ranges from 22°C to 32°C. The WMO has declared Bangkok to be one of the world's hottest cities. The country is hot and humid due to its tropical location. Thailand is dominated by the tropical monsoon; the seasonal variation of winds. The monsoon is caused by alternating high and low pressure cells over Central Asia. During the rainy season, from May to November, the south-west monsoon brings moisture-laden winds from the Gulf of Thailand. The north-east monsoon winds bring dry air at other times of the year. Temperatures average 30°C and humidity is always high. Rainfall ranges from 100 to 150 cm/year with the heaviest falls on the coast and decreasing landward.

The best time to visit is when the both temperature and rainfall are lowest; ie between November and March.

Population

In the December 1993 Census, there were 58.3 million people in Thailand (in November 1996, the population officially passed 60 million). Eighty per cent of the population are Thai, however, within the country there is a rich ethnic diversity of other cultures including Mon, Khmer, Lao, Chinese, Malay, Persian and Indian. As many as 500,000 of the population are members of various hilltribes. The growth rate is now 1.2%, down from 3.3% in 1970.

Urban working and commercial classes have been dominated by people of Chinese ethnicity although this is changing. There are about 5 million people of Chinese descent in the country, many of whom run the country's largest corporations. About 2 million Thais living mainly in the south, profess to be Islamic.

About 80% of the population is connected in some way with agriculture which, in varying degrees, influences, and is influenced by, the religious ceremonies and festivals that help make Thailand such a distinctive country. With economic development this is changing as more people move into manufacturing and service industries.

The family is still important to Thai life, especially in the countryside. Young people pay respect to their elders and their religious leaders. Life expectancy is about 69 years and 23% of the population are younger than 15. When Thai woman marry a foreigner it is assumed they automatically take their husband's nationality and she loses most rights as a Thai citizen.

Education

The literacy rate is about 90% and compulsory education has been raised to a minimum schooling of 9 years, thus extending leaving levels to a minimum of 15 years of age. Rural districts lag behind urban areas especially with the numbers of students who attain tertiary qualifications. There were about 800,000 tertiary students in the mid 1990s.

There are several international schools in Bangkok for German (ph 258 7361), French (ph 287 1599) and English (ph 584 6046) speaking expatriates.

Language

Thai is the language of the land although many people understand a little English, especially in Bangkok and other tourist destinations. The Thai alphabet comprises 44 letters and the language is tonal with five different tones.

When using Thai, it is common for males to add *krup* and females *kaa* to the end of sentences. Thais, like many Asians, have trouble pronouncing 'r' and 'w' which may become 'l' and 'v', respectively. If you want to be understood, it is better to use a few variations on what you are trying to say. By the way, foreigners are known as *farangs* which, of course, will be pronounced *falang*.

Some basic words of Thai will ensure visitors have a more meaningful holiday. There are many places to learn Thai in Bangkok; most are listed in the daily papers but here are some to contact: *Nisa Thai Language Centre* (ph 286 9323) and *Union Language School* (ph 233 4482).

Here are some words and phrases expressed phonetically:

Hello or good morning	*sawasdee krup/kaa*
goodbye	*la gon*
does anybody speak English?	*mei krai pood pasa ang-grit dai bang mai?*
please speak slowly	*prohd phoot cha-cha*
I do not understand	*mai kao chai*
do you understand?	*kai chai mai?*
thank you	*kop koon krup/kaa*
never mind	*mai pen rai*
how are you?	*sabai dee roo?*
fine thanks	*sabai dee krup/kaa*
I cannot speak Thai	*phoot Thai mai dai*
where is the restroom?	*hong nam yoo tai nai?*
how much is it?	*nee tao-rai?*
what is this?	*nee arai?*
very expensive	*pang maag*
bill please	*gep taang krup/kaa* or *check bin*
good luck	*kor hai chok dee!*
sorry or excuse me	*kor thoad*
I need a doctor	*tong karn mor ma raksa*

Numbers

one	*neung*
two	*sawng*
three	*sarm*
four	*see*
five	*haa*
six	*hok*
seven	*chet*
eight	*paet*
nine	*kow*
ten	*sip*
eleven	*sip-et*
twelve	*sip-sawng*
twenty	*yee-sip*
thirty	*sarm-sip*
one hundred	*neung-roy*

two hundred	*sawng-roy*
one thousand	*neung-pun*
ten thousand	*neung-mern*
one million	*neung-lan*

Religion

Buddhism

Buddhism is the state religion, however the country permits religious freedom. As many as 90% of the population profess to be Buddhists but there are sizeable minorities of Muslims (6%), Christians (2%), Hindus and Sikhs. According to the Thai constitution, the King is a Buddhist and the upholder of religions. The Sangha Council is the governing body of Thailand's Buddhist monkhood. The Buddhist philosophy followed in the country is Theravada or Hinayana Buddhism.

Buddhism first appeared in Thailand in the 3rd century BC at Nakhon Pathom after the Indian Buddhist Emperor, Asoka, sent missionaries to South-East Asia to spread the faith. It was not until the 13th century that it became significant.

Buddhists believe that everything has a previous existence. Buddhists who have reached enlightenment pass into *nirvana,* a state of heavenly bliss. Everything is in a constant process of transition (new things become old things just as old things become new things). The lotus flower, seen all over Thailand, is associated with the Lord Buddha who is often seen standing on an open lotus flower. In Buddhism, it stands for purity and divine birth as the flower begins its life growing in impure mud and rises to blossom as a beautiful flower. The lotus plant is cooked and eaten in many different ways. The flowers are used as religious offerings. Candles, joss sticks and food (as offerings) are central to Buddhism and can be seen outside most *wats.*

The *wat* was, and still is in most cases, the centre of each Thai community. Traditionally it was where people (usually males) were educated and where they attended rites and festivals. Most Thai families have at least one member who has studied Buddhism in a monastery. It has long been customary for males over 20 years old to be temporarily ordained as monks for periods ranging from three days to three months. Thereavada Buddhism calls upon men to voluntarily become priests for at least 15 days in their life; often during the rainy season. This is a period when all monks stay inside monasteries. Permanent monks uphold a solemn vow of chastity.

Nearly every large building in the country has a temple for making offerings to Buddha. It is common to see people praying here and making food, lotus flower and incense offerings. Each morning the bare-footed monks can be seen walking single-file through the streets seeking alms. Buddhists place food in the monks' alms bowls.

Most visitors to Thailand will visit at least one *wat* during their stay. There are some terms which will make such a visit more rewarding. A *wat* is a large walled compound that encloses several buildings. One of these will be a *bot* or prayer hall where monks are ordained into the priesthood. Sermons are delivered and believers pray in a *viharn*. *Chedis*, or *stupas*, contain the remains of wealthy donors to the *wat*. A *sala* is an open sided shelter for resting. The library is called a *ho trai* and meditation rooms are called *guti*. *Yaksa* (demons) guard the entrances to *wats*; *kinara* (half-human, half-bird objects) and *singha* (lions) are also found in temples.

Chinese Religions

Many Chinese are followers of Confucianism, Taoism or Chinese Mahayana Buddhism. Taoism teaches meditation and magic to gain wealth, happiness, immortality and health.

Confucianism pays attention to the veneration of ancestors, especially to one's parents.

Animism

Many of the *chao khao*, or mountain people (hilltribes), believe in ancestor worshipping (animism). Each hilltribe has specific religious characteristics and a short explanation here would not do justice to their deeply held beliefs. Spirit houses inside homes, and spirit gates around villages, are common. They should not be disturbed by visitors. It is most appropriate that, if in doubt, leave it alone. Not all hilltribe people are animists as some have converted to Christianity.

Islam

Many parts of Southern Thailand are more Islamic than Buddhist. Islam was introduced by Arab traders from what is now known as Malaysia, during the 13th century. As many as 2 million Thais follow the Islamic faith, principally Sunni.

Others
Approximately one per cent of Thais are Christians from many different denominations. Christmas is celebrated throughout the country but more as a commercialised marketing ploy by large Bangkok department stores than as a religious observance.

Festivals and Holidays
Many festivals are associated either with religion, the rice growing cycle, or in honour of Thai kings. Some occur on fixed dates, while others are determined by the lunar calender. Many are national or local holidays.

Makka Bucha - full moon day, February - National Holiday.
This commemorates the time when 1250 disciples gathered to hear Buddha preach. Offering food to monks and freeing captive birds and fish is interspersed with sermons. Throughout the country, after sunset, monks lead their followers in a candlelight procession around the *wats*.

Flower Festival - second Friday, Saturday and Sunday in February.
This annual event, celebrated in Chiang Mai, features displays and floral floats at a time when the flowers of the province are in full bloom.

Phra Buddha Baht Festival - February.
 Held at the Shrine of Buddha's Footprint in Saraburi. There are many celebrations involving music and drama.

Pattaya Festival - early April.
  This Thai seaside resort comes to life with processions, fireworks, parties and beach activities.

Chakri Day - April 6 - National Holiday.
Commemorates the founder of the present Chakri Dynasty, King Rama 1. Thailand's present monarch, King Bhumibol Adulyadej, is the 9th Chakri King.

Songkran Festival-April 13/15-National Holiday.
The traditional Thai New Year, Songkran is celebrated throughout the country with lots of water throwing. Images of Buddha are washed and young people pay respect to their elders and to monks. Ultimately, everyone gets refreshingly soaked during the height of the dry season.

Labour Day - May 1 - National Holiday.

Coronation Day - May 5 - National Holiday.
The holiday celebrates the coronation of the King.

Visakha Puja (Wisakha Bucha) - Full Moon - May - National Holiday.
This is the holiest of all Buddhist days, marking Buddha's birth, enlightenment and death. Ceremonies are performed at *wats*.

Royal Ploughing Ceremony - early May.
The ceremony marks the official beginning of the annual rice-planting cycle. Brahman rituals and ceremonies are presided over by the King at Sanam Luang across the road from *Wat Phra Kaew* in Bangkok.

Rocket Festival.
It is held annually over the second weekend in May prior to the monsoon. Villagers build gigantic skyrockets for firing into the sky to ensure bountiful rains. The festival includes processions, dances and the launching of rockets on the second day of the festival. It is mainly celebrated in the north-east.

Asanhabucha - Full Moon Day - July - National Holiday.
This marks Buddha's first sermon to his first five disciples and introduces *Khao Phansa*, the annual three month rains retreat where all Buddhist monks must stay inside their monasteries to study and meditate. It is considered the 'Buddhist lent'.

Candle Festival - July.
Khao Phansa is celebrated in the north-east with the Candle Festival; Ubon has the most elaborate festival.

Queen's Birthday - August 12 - National Holiday.
Celebrations are held throughout the country but focus on
Bangkok. Many buildings, especially around the Royal Palace
are illuminated at night.

Ok Phansa - usually October.
Ok Phansa celebrates the end of *Phansa* and introduces the
Kathin period when Buddhists present monks with new robes
and other necessary items. It also marks the official end of the
rainy season and is celebrated with country fairs and boat races.

Vegetarian Festival - October.
The festival is a nine day celebration held in Phuket and
neighbouring towns.

Chulalongkorn Festival - October 23 - National Holiday.
This holiday honours Thailand's most beloved King, Rama V.
Many people lay wreaths at his statue in Bangkok's Royal Plaza.
November marks the beginning of the cool season, coincides
with low farming activity and is the time for innumerable
temple fairs. The best known are at Bangkok's Golden Mount
and the Phra Pathom Chedi Fair at Nakhon Pathom.

Loi Krathong - full moon eve, November.
This is one of the country's traditional festivals when, under the
full moon, *krathongs* (small lotus-shaped, banana-leaf boats) are
floated on rivers and waterways. These small boats contain a
lighted candle, glowing incense, a flower and a small coin to
honour the water spirits and to wash away the sins of the past
year. Sukothai and Chiang Mai have special ceremonies.

Elephant Round-Up - third weekend in November.
In Surin, north-east Thailand, some 100 elephants participate in
this popular event. There are traditional folk dances and
ceremonies as well as events featuring elephants. There is a
spectacular re-enactment of an ancient war elephant parade.
River Kwai Bridge Week - late November/early December.

Events feature a brilliant light and sound show at the famous
bridge site in Kanchanaburi. Archaeological and historical

Monks at Vimanmek Palace, Bangkok

exhibitions, folk culture performances and train rides are some of the main attractions.

King's Birthday - December 5 - National Holiday.
On December 3, the elite Royal Guards swear allegiance to the King in Bangkok's Royal Plaza. This precedes the King's birthday, two days later, when festivities occur throughout the Kingdom.

Constitution Day - December Ten - National Holiday.
The year's last national holiday is mostly devoted to private celebrations.
New Year's Day - December 31-January One - National Holiday.

Other celebrations are held throughout the country at a regional level. Festivals such as Christmas are also celebrated but are not holidays. Various national groups in the country also hold there are own festivities for national days and specific celebrations. Chinese New Year in January or February is one such holiday when many businesses will close despite it not being an official holiday. The Chinese Moon Festival in September is a widely celebrated festival.

Entry Regulations
All visitors to Thailand must have a valid passport and, for most, an onward ticket to another country. Almost all foreigners can stay in Thailand for up to 30 days without a visa. Some other types of visas include transit (30 days), tourist (60 days), non-immigrant (90 days) and immigrant. Visitors who want to stay longer than 30 days can apply to a Thai Embassy by sending their passport, two copies of a completed application form and passport photos. New transit visas cost B300 and tourist visas B500 (multiple entry, B1,000). For visa extensions while in the country, visitors should contact the Immigration Division in Soi Suan Phlu, off Sathon Tai Road, Bangkok, ph 287 3101. If you overstay your visa the officials will probably charge you 100B for each extra day.

The departure tax is B200 for international flights and B20 for domestic flights. The departure tax for flights to and from Koh Samui, where *Bangkok Airways* operate a private airport, is B100.

Customs Procedures

It is illegal to import narcotics, obscene literature (a bit odd considering the number of massage parlours in the country), cash in excess of US$10,000 (unless declared), firearms, piranha (yes, you had better believe it!), and some fruit. One camera with five unused rolls of film are also allowed, although I never heard of anyone being busted trying to 'smuggle' film in. There are many warning signs on the import of drugs and you only have to read the daily newspapers to know these are not idle threats. Legally every incoming traveller should have funds to support themselves; usually about US$125. Visitors can bring in any amount of foreign currency but must declare amounts exceeding US$10,000. The import or export of Thai baht is limited.

Embassies and Consulates

Over 70 countries have representatives in Thailand, here are some which are located in Bangkok:

Australia	37 Sathorn Tai Road, ph 287 2680, fax 287 2589.
Canada	11 and 12th Floors, Boonmitr Building, B4 138 Silom Road, ph 237 4125.
France	35 Charoen Krung 36 Road, ph 266 8250.
Germany	9 Sathon Tai Road, ph 2132331.
Italy	389 Nang Linchi Road, Tung Mahamek, ph 2854090.
Japan	1674/4 New Phetchaburi Road, ph 252 6151.
Lao PDR	193 Sathon Tai Road, ph 286 9244.
Malaysia	35 Sathon Tai Road, ph 286 1190.
Myanmar	132 Sathon Nua Road, ph 233 2237.
Netherlands	106 Wireless Road, ph 254 7701.
Singapore	129 Sathon Tai Road, ph 286 2111.
United Kingdom	1031 Wireless Road, ph 253 0191.
USA	95 Wireless Road, ph 252 5040.
Vietnam	83/1 Wireless Road, ph 251 5835.

Money

Baht, in the form of coins and notes, is the basic unit of currency. Some of the coins are difficult to distinguish as there are new and old types that look different. The bank notes come in denominations of B10 (brown), B20 (green), B50 (blue), B100 (red), B500 (purple) and B1,000 (grey). Value Added Tax (VAT) of 7% is added to many sales and services. This effectively becomes 7.7% in many places as a 10% service charge is often added first.

Banks

Local banks were once protected from international competition, as foreign banks were only able to open one office. In mid-1994, the situation changed allowing them to open provincial branches. Foreign currency accounts can be opened at Thai banks as long as it can be shown that the money originated from outside the country.

Banks are open Mon-Fri 8am-3.30pm. Money exchanges operated by many banks, especially in tourist destinations, have longer operating hours.

The baht value fluctuates and is closely linked to the US$. Some approximate exchange rates are:

US Dollar	26 Baht
Japanese Yen	21
Hong Kong Dollar	3
Malaysian Ringgit	10
Australian Dollar	20
New Zealand Dollar	18
Canadian Dollar	19
British Pound	41
German Mark	16
Swiss Franc	18

Some leading Thai banks include: *Bank of Ayudhya, Bangkok Bank, Krung Thai Bank, Siam Commercial Bank, Thai Military Bank* and *Thai Farmers Bank.* Some leading overseas banks represented in the country include: *ANZ Bank, National Australian Bank* (Australia), *Bank of America, Citibank, Chase Manhattan Bank* (USA), *Standard Chartered Bank* (UK), *Bank of Tokyo, Mitsui* (Japan) and *Hong Kong and Shanghai Bank* (Hong Kong).

Credit Cards

Most credit cards can be used in the country. In some small outlets a surcharge may apply. Whether this is legal or not doesn't matter; they make the rules. In some places this could be up to 6%. When bartering, don't expect the retailer to accept a credit card; if you want the cheapest price, use cash.

For lost credit cards ring the following numbers: *American Express,* ph 273 0033; *Diners Club,* ph 236 7455; *Visa, ph* 273 1199; and *MasterCard,* ph 246 0300 or call to the USA, 001-1-314-275 6690. Be careful of credit card fraud in the country and don't let the card out of your sight when making transactions. Making several illegal swipes of cards is becoming a more frequent practice with unscrupulous retailers. In some cases, blank forms with your credit card details are used later to purchase goods. There have been some reports of credit cards, deposited in safe deposit boxes, being fraudulent used. Be careful!

Communications

Post
Post Offices are open Mon-Fri 8.30am-4.30pm, and Sat 8.30am-12.30pm. The airmail postcard rate is B9. Bangkok General Post Office operates a Poste Restante counter if you have to have mail sent to you from overseas. It should be addressed to you c/o General Post Office, Poste Restante, Bangkok, Thailand. You will be required to produce your passport to collect the mail. Mail can also be sent care of your embassy or via *American Express* if you are a cardholder.

Telephones and Faxes
Thailand's country code is 065. For Directory Assistance, dial 13 in Bangkok, 183 out of Bangkok, and for long distance, dial 100. To make an IDD call, dial 001, the country code, area code and phone number. Local calls, at public phone booths, are B1 (smaller coins only) for 3 minutes. From shops and hotels the charge could be B5 to B10. Some hotels add hefty surcharges for international calls, possibly up to B100. This may be added even if you charge the call to a credit card. Long distance public phones are blue. Phonecards are also available.

Couriers
All the leading courier companies are represented in the major cities and their network extends throughout the country. Courier companies include: *TNT Skypack,* ph 249 0242; *Federal Express, DHL,* ph 207 0600, and *UPS.*

Newspapers and Magazines

The media was virtually a state and military monopoly, but this has changed with more privatization and independence. There are over 50 newspapers, and surveys suggest that readership increases are some of the fastest in the world. Most local papers cost B15.

There are four major local English newspaper published in Bangkok; *The Nation, World News, Bangkok Post* and *Thailand Times. The Nation*, 44 Moo 10, Bangna-Trad Highway, Prakanong. *The Bangkok Post*, 136 Na Ranong Road, off Sunthorn Kosa Road, Klong Toey, Bangkok, ph 240 3700, fax 240 3790 (the paper is also available in postfax and postvoice computerised systems, ph 671 3130). *Thailand Times*, 88 Baromrajchonnee Road, Taling Chan, Bangkok, ph 434 0330, fax 424 6797. *The Asian Wall Street Journal* and *International Herald Tribune* are also available.

The *Far East Economic Review* (GPO Box 160, Hong Kong, ph 852-2508 4300, fax 852-2503 1553) and *Asiaweek* (ph 852-2508 2688, fax 852-2571 0916) are available throughout the country and provide up-to-date information on developments in Thailand and its regional neighbours.

Radio

There are about 400 radio stations and most of these transmit in Thai, although in Bangkok there are a few English speaking stations. Stations to tune into in Bangkok include: *Gold FM 99.5, Smooth 105 FM* and *Smile Radio Four 107 FM*. If you are staying in Pattaya listen into 'Pattaya By the Sea', FM radio at 107.75. On the shortwave network there is *BBC World Service, Radio Australia* (satellites that can receive ABTV can be used for *Radio Australia*), *Voice of America, Radio New Zealand, SBC Singapore* and *Radio Canada* (*Metro* magazine lists the different frequencies).

Television

There is an extensive network throughout the country. Satellite TV from Hong Kong, UK, Australia and USA is available in many hotels, airport lounges, public places and private homes.

Health and Safety

For something as important as health, travellers should consult both a doctor and a dentist with experience in tropical and travel medicine, and not rely upon the following for their health needs. Prior to any trip to a destination like Thailand, travellers should assess their general health and consult a doctor about essential vaccinations. In addition, travellers should ensure they have adequate health and travel insurance. Travel agents can advise on these policies.

Diseases with the highest mortality rates in the country are diarrhoea, sexually-transmitted diseases, malaria and dengue fever. Travellers could be exposed to some of these. Access to safe drinking water is limited especially in rural areas. The doctor to patient ratio is 1:4,360.

While no vaccines are 100% effective, doctors recommend certain treatments prior to travelling to places like Thailand. Recommended vaccines are: BCG for tuberculosis (a skin test is done first), oral polio boost, typhoid, tetanus, and gamma globulin or the new hepatitis A 'havrix' and hepatitis B vaccine. Additional vaccines may be necessary for those at risk. These include; rabies, Japanese encephalitis and meningitis. An extended series of vaccinations for rabies will provide travellers with good pre-exposure protection.

Doctors will also suggest that lifestyle and diet will assist in staying healthy. With food, there is a good principle to follow: *boil it, cook it, peel it or leave it.* Others would disagree saying that you miss out on many delicious Thai foods and experiences, but be warned, be careful and enjoy yourself. Because of the heat, many people lose body fluids, so keep drinking clean water at the rate of 2 to 3 litres/day. Avoid the heat of the day, wear a hat, sunglasses, sunscreen and appropriate clothing (both for the climate and the sensitivities of the culture).

It is useful to pack a small first aid kit, as many medicines are not easily available to travellers in Thailand. A doctor can give advice. Some medical services and travel companies have such kits already prepared. The kit should include: rehydration salts (diarrhoea), *Loperamide* or *Immodium* (diarrhoea), insect repellent, water disinfectant such as *Micropur*, eye drops, antiseptic lotion, antifungal powder, a general antibiotic and band aids. A penknife should be kept in close proximity. Buying a mosquito net in Thailand may also be a good idea if you think you will be at risk (eg trekking in northern Thailand).

In Asia, and many other destinations it is best to err on the side of safety with many things. Look in a Bangkok *klong* to understand the problems. Diarrhoea, cholera, amoebic dysentery and typhoid are all water-borne diseases which could present problems in parts of Thailand.

One of the most common forms of illness faced by travellers in Thailand is diarrhoea. This is mostly due to *Escherichia coli (E. coli)* a common bacterium present in most countries, but in different strains. Mostly it will last two to three days and solid foods should be avoided. Fluids should be maintained and possibly rehydration salts taken. Basically, your body is trying to get rid of a germ and this natural function should be encouraged. Severe diarrhoea requires medical assistance.

Other common problems faced by some travellers include fungal diseases (tinea), travel sickness and jet lag. With travel sickness, known suffers are urged to travel on a lightly full stomach, avoid reading while travelling and to take recommended medication. *Hyoscine dermal discs* applied to the skin are effective. Jet lag is a problem with some people and could affect the early stages of a Thai holiday. Some pre and post planning will assist as will certain activities during the flight. Sleep well before the flight and don't leave packing until the last minute. During the flight avoid stimulants (alcohol and coffee), drink other fluids regularly, eat sparingly and only healthy food (order specific meals from the airline), wear loose clothing, sleep and move around at other times. In Thailand, take it easy for the first day and go to bed at your normal time or slightly earlier.

There are hospitals throughout the country that offer different degrees of service and expertise. In Bangkok, the following hospitals should be noted just in case you have to visit them in an emergency: *Bangkok General Hospital,* ph 318 0066, and *Bangkok Christian Hospital,* ph 233 6981. English speaking dentists are available at: *Siam Dental Clinic,* ph 203 0311, and *Ploenchit Dental Clinic,* ph 251 1567.

Malaria and Dengue Fever
Prevention is far better than cure and the point of the holiday is

to enjoy and discover Thailand and not to become too paranoid about events that may not eventuate. However, you need to be aware that malaria and dengue fever can kill. Avoid contact with mosquitos by staying in places with insect screens and or sleeping nets. Use an insect repellent and wear protective clothing, ie light-coloured, long-sleeved shirts and long pants. There is a variety of malaria prophylaxis available and a doctor should be consulted.

Many doctors suggest travellers take *Deoxycycline*, a new anti-malarial drug, at 100 mg/day. In parts of the country, the resistance of the most deadly malaria parasite, *Plasmodium falciparum*, to traditional methods of treatment is increasing at an alarming rate. Some studies suggest *Chloroquine* and *Sulfadoxine-pyremethamine* appear to be totally ineffective for treatment in these areas.

Sex and Drugs

AIDS and HIV are problems in Thailand. AIDS was first reported in the country in 1984, initially among the homosexual community but then among injecting drug users who were principally heterosexual. The risk of both diseases spreading throughout the community is increased by the high numbers of prostitutes. Infection rates amongst prostitutes may be as high as 10%. A 1990 survey found that 2% of men could be HIV positive. The total numbers could be as high as 700,000 and of these, some 24,000 may have AIDS. After initially denying the problem existed, or claiming it only affected sub-cultures within the community, the government has started to do something about the problem. Some predictions suggest the Thai economy will be seriously affected if they go unchecked.

Sections of the tourism industry are clearly concerned about AIDS/HIV, prostitution, child prostitution, sex tours and paedophilia. The number of VD clinics on the streets of Bangkok suggest that prostitution and its associated side effects are a problem in the city.

Thailand is one of the access points for exporting opium from nearby Myanmar. The latter produces 2,400 tonnes annually. About 60% of the opium consumed in the USA comes from Myanmar. The bulk of this production comes from the Shan state of Myanmar controlled by Khun Sa, a heavily armed drug warlord with a 15,000 strong army. Thailand has been trying to close down his and other operations for decades.

Drugs
Recreational drugs are prohibited in Thailand and the penalty for possession of hard drugs is many years spent in rather unpleasant gaols. If that is not the way you wish to spend your time in Thailand, don't carry any parcels for anyone regardless of how persistent or friendly they may seem. You only have to read the newspapers to see that people get caught nearly every day. If you go on a hilltribe trek you will most likely encounter opium smokers. It is illegal to participate in these activities, despite what you may be told.

Customs and Etiquette
Survival in any country is dependent upon an understanding of the customs. Being predominantly a Buddhist country, all Buddhist images (regardless of size or condition) are sacred. No Buddhist images are allowed to be taken out of the country. People visiting Buddhist *wats* (the Thai word for temples) are expected to dress respectfully. In some *wats* visitors will be given additional clothes to wear if it is deemed theirs are inappropriate (shorts, for example, are unacceptable in most temples but particularly the *Grand Palace* in Bangkok). Shoes must be removed before entering a hall of Buddhist worship and most Thai homes. It is considered inappropriate to show the soles of feet to anybody. Try and tuck them under you if you have to sit on the ground.

Woman must never come in direct contact with monks, this means they must not hand anything to a monk. If woman have something for a monk, they can place this near the monk and he will collect it. When males give anything to a monk it should be done gracefully with two hands (in Thailand, and most of Asia, business cards should also be handed over with both hands).

It is appropriate to remain slightly behind a monk if walking with one.

The King and Queen are highly revered by their subjects and Thais will not tolerate foreigners talking about them disrespectfully. When the national anthem is played (eg in cinemas) everyone is expected to stand. I have seen busy train stations stop during the twice daily playing of the national anthem at 8am and 4pm.

Close public contact between the opposite sexes is considered inappropriate. While some foreign females may sunbake topless on tourist beaches, it is not part of Thai customs and while nothing may be said, it is considered disrespectful. Do not expect to get served by hotel staff.

Traditionally, Thais greet each other with a *wai* which is done by placing the hands together at chest level as if one were praying. Watch what others do, particularly *Thai Airlines* female flight attendants; it is appropriate to reciprocate.

Loosing one's temper in Thailand will get you nowhere as Thais really have no response except bewilderment. Explaining to people what you want is difficult enough when you cannot speak Thai, but yelling and screaming will achieve little.

In the cities, and even in many rural areas, people are impeccably dressed, just look at the uniforms Bangkok bus collectors wear. Clothes seem whiter than white and one wonders what miracle chemicals washing powder manufacturers use. If you have official meetings to attend, you will be expected to be equally well-dressed.

Environment

The natural environment of Thailand is under continual pressure. Few tourists will see natural forests while they are in the country, even the hills of northern Thailand are mostly covered by secondary forests. The original rainforests, being over 150 million years old, were some of the oldest forests in the world. Other major forest types in the country include mangroves, monsoon and bamboo. Teak trees (*Tectona grandis*) are some the most valued and exploited trees in the country.

There are many animals living in forests including gibbons, elephants, monkeys, deer, wild cattle, birds and reptiles.

The rapid economic growth in the country has occurred at an environmental cost. Environmental awareness is, however, increasing and environmental protection is becoming more important. Environmental politics became mobilised in the country after a successful campaign against the Nam Choan Dam in the mid-1980s.

Environmental awareness developed after resource depletion

and pollution reached dangerous levels. Deforestation is a good example. Forest cover declined from 53% of total land coverage in 1961 to 28% in 1988. This led to a logging ban in the late 1980s which was good news for environmentalists and the forests of Thailand, but bad news for neighbouring countries. Thai loggers simply moved their operations to these countries. It is generally accepted that the Khmer Rouge insurgency against government forces in neighbouring Cambodia has been financed by logging operations that directly benefit Thailand. In response to its domestic forest problems, the Thai Government launched a reafforestation program in 1994. This aims to revegetate a million hectares of Thai forests. Past reafforestation efforts have, in many cases, used imported eucalyptus species which have only created new environmental problems.

Most wildlife is protected in Thailand, although visitors may wonder about this from the products on sale in some markets. These shops exist because people buy the products. If you find the trade in endangered species abhorrent, don't buy the goods. This will contribute to forcing the traders out of business. Many animal products are not allowed to be imported by customs officials into other countries, so you may only be wasting your money as they will be confiscated. Turtle shell, snake products, crocodile skins and ivory products are prohibited imports in many countries.

Some commercial fishing, prawn farms and tourism have had a detrimental impact upon coastal areas such as coral reefs and mangrove ecosystems.

The quality of life in urban areas has been affected by economic growth. About 15% of the total Thai population lives in Bangkok which is expanding quicker than authorities can provide minimum services. For example, waste water released from houses along the Chao Phraya River accounts for most of the river's pollution. Some of the *klongs* (canals) are now black and emit foul gases when churned up by passing longtail boats. While the country is not highly urbanised, the urban growth rate is increasing rapidly. Air quality levels are very poor in Bangkok and masked traffic police are now a common sight. Tests on some school children in the city have shown drops in IQ levels which some attribute to increased lead in the atmosphere (lead is an additive in some petroleum products). Despite the

Some basic environmental principles
if practised by all visitors, will assist in maintaining Thailand's uniqueness, for future visitors. The following will help:

1. try to take nothing but photographs and leave nothing but footprints.

2. avoid buying souvenirs made from plant and animal products especially endangered species.

3. do not damage corals when diving, swimming or snorkelling.

4. seek out and use the services of tour operators who are environmentally aware and sympathetic to the needs of local people.

5. buy products and services provided by local people.

introduction of lead-free petrol and catalytic converters in new cars, the Pollution Control Department doesn't see any reduction in the city's air pollution problems.

Bangkok's celebrated traffic not only creates problems of congestion but generates air pollution as well as wasting valuable fuel resources. As part of the process of increasing Thai consumerism, most people see a car as a visible sign of wealth and success. Every third resident in Bangkok owns a vehicle and each day about 1300 more are added to the 2 million (there are higher estimates of 3 million) already locked into traffic jams. Solutions to the traffic problem are constant topics of conversation in the city.

While new transport systems and freeways are being planned and constructed, many feel that traffic jams are merely relocating the problems and not actually solving them.

City authorities (there are 30 traffic management authorities!) must wonder how much longer this situation will last before the whole city is one massive gridlock.

For more information about the environmental situation in the country contact Wildlife Fund Thailand, 251/88-90 Phaholyothin Road, Bangkhen, Bangkok 10220, ph 521 3435, fax 552 6083.

Miscellaneous

Time Zone
Local time is GMT + 7 hours.

Business Hours
Government office hours are Mon-Fri 8.30am-4.30pm. Most offices operate a five day week. Department stores in big cities open 10am-8pm. Most other shops are open 8am-9pm. Shop hours are usually displayed in shop windows.

Bargaining
Apart from department stores and Bangkok boutiques, it is acceptable to negotiate (barter) the price of goods in most other stores. It helps to have a rough idea of what you should pay, especially if it is an expensive item. Knowing a little Thai also helps as does shopping with a Thai friend if you have contacts in the country. Hotel staff are usually helpful in giving you an idea of what to pay. Don't expect big discounts if you use traveller's cheques or credit cards, in fact, you may even pay a surcharge.

Church Services
Apart from Buddhist *wats* there are opportunities for members of other faiths to worship their God or Gods. In Bangkok there are many places of worship. Most hotels have copies of the Bible and Koran available. The following places of worship are found in Bangkok: *Christ Church* (Anglican, ph 234 3634); *Calvary Baptist Church* (ph 251 8278); *Assumption Cathedral* (Catholic, ph 234 8556), *Holy Redeemer Catholic Church* (ph 256 6305, Soi Ruam Rudee, Mass: Sat 5.30pm, Sun 7.30, 8.30, 9.45, 11am, 5.30pm); *International Church* (non-denominational, ph 253 3353); *Jewish Association of Thailand* (ph 258 2195); *Mormon* (ph 258 3585); *Sha-Roh-Tal Islam Mosque* (ph 328 8950); *Baha'i* (ph 252 5355); and *Seventh Day Adventist* (ph 282 1100).

Clothing
Light loose cotton clothes are best and nylon should be avoided. Jumpers may be necessary during the cooler months in the north of the country. Most dress is informal although business

appointments and fine restaurant dining will require a tie and maybe a jacket. Thai customs dictate that certain attire is required in temples, government offices and on beaches. Respect for these customs will be appreciated by your Thai hosts.

Electricity
Local supply is 220 volts, 50-cycles. The plugs used are different to many other countries so bring an adaptor if you use an essential appliance, such as a lap-top computer.

Emergencies
In Bangkok, emergency numbers are: Police, Fire and Ambulance, ph 191 and 123. Additional number for the Fire Brigade is 199, and for the Bangkok Ambulance, 252 2171. For the Tourist Police, ph 195 or 1699 (in Bangkok).

Insurance
Visitors to Thailand would be well advised to take out travel insurance. As always, it is worth reading the fine print as things you may assume are covered, may not be, under certain circumstances. Expensive items may have to be itemised and a higher premium paid. The replacement value of cameras for instance, is often limited.

Many visitors hire vehicles to access destinations on Phuket and Koh Samui. In such cases it would be a good idea to check the fine print in an insurance policy to see if you are covered in the event of an accident. Many may specify conditions under which you will not be covered.

Metric System
Weights, measurements and distances used in the country are based upon the metric system.

Tipping
Tipping is not an accepted custom in Thailand but most hotels and large restaurants will automatically add 10% service fee regardless of the quality of the service.

Travelling With Children
Travelling with children has its own special complications. Your relationship with your child could be tested after the tenth

Bangkok *wat*, despite its uniqueness and spectacular atmosphere and architecture.

Bangkok is well-equipped to entertain children in familiar Western fashion as well as some traditional Thai ways. There are some theme parks within close proximity to the city, including: *Muang Boran* or *Ancient City*, ph 323 9252 (featuring a miniature Thailand); and *Siam Park*, ph 517 0075 (a park full of water activities, amusement park and zoo, just one hour from Bangkok). Then there is the *Dusit Zoo, Museum of Science and Planetarium*, ph 392 5952 (hands on displays for star-gazers); *Snake Farm*, ph 252 0161, as well as safari and elephant parks. There are large open spaces at *Sanum Luang* and *Lumpini Park*. *Sanum Luang* is particularly popular for kite-flying and a wonderful opportunity for photo-taking parents while the kids fly kites.

Bambi (Bangkok Mothers and Babies International) has a support group for mothers. They can be contacted through the *British Club*, ph 261 3960. Paediatricians to contact include: Dr Buppha, ph 392 0011, and Dr Voravee, ph 233 2610.

Most of the large department stores have thoughtfully established play areas to keep children happy while their parents are distracted. Getting children to and from such places in strollers is near impossible due to the obstacles along footpaths and a backpack baby carrier is recommended. Due to the heat and humidity, movement through the city should be restricted to the cooler parts of the day.

If all else fails to keep children entertained, there are always the playgrounds attached to *McDonalds*!.

Travel Information

How to Get There

By Air

There are four main international airports; Bangkok (Don Muang), Chiang Mai, Hat Yai and Phuket. International departure tax is B200. See *Bangkok, How To Get There*, for specific details on airport facilities and arrival procedure. At last count, about 70 international carriers flew into and out of Bangkok. The national carrier is *Thai Airways* which serves over 70 international destinations on four continents. It is also the principal domestic carrier. Membership for their frequent flyer program is free and covers all class of travel so joining it is recommended.

Bangkok Airways, Queen Sirikit National Convention Centre, New Rajjadapisek Road, Klong Toey, ph 229 3456, fax 229 3454, operates services to Koh Samui, Hua Hin, Phuket and U-Tapao (Pattaya). In late 1995 it began services to Ranong in south-west Thailand. It also increased its carrying capacity with a new fleet of ATR 72 planes. There are big plans for expansion so see your travel agent for new destinations.

On-Line Airlines	Airline Code	Phone
Aeroflot(1)	SU	535 1111
Air France(2)	AF	233 9477
Air India(1)	AI	235 0557
Air Koryo(1)	JS	234 2805
Air Lanka(1)	UL	236 9292
Air New Zealand(1)	NZ	237 1560
Alitalia(2)	AZ	233 4000
All Nippon Airways(2)	NH	238 5121

On-Line Airlines	Airline Code	Phone
Aom French(2)	IW	255 6840
Asiana Airlines(1)	QZ	260 7700
Balkan Bulgarian Airlines(1)	LZ	253 3063
Biman Bangladesh Airlines(1)	BG	233 3896
British Airways(2)	BA	236 8655
Canadian Airlines(2)	CP	251 4521
Cathay Pacific(2)	CX	263 0606
CAAC(2)	CA	235 1880
China Airlines(1)	CI	253 4241
China Southern Airlines(1)	CZ	235 5250
China Yunnan Airlines(1)	3Q	216 3067
Czechoslovak Airlines(1)	OK	253 4045
Dragonair	KA	076 215 734
Egyptair(1)	MS	231 0505
El Al Israel Airlines(1)	LY	671 6145
Emirates(1)	EK	260 7400
Ethiopian Airlines(1)	ET	233 8951
Eva Air(2)	BR	535 3531
Federal Express (couriers)	FM	235 3564
Finnair(2)	AY	251 5012
Garuda Indonesia(2)	GA	288 6470
Gulf Air(2)	GF	254 7931
Indian Airlines(2)	IC	233 3890
Japan Airlines(JAL)(1)	JL	274 1411
KLM Royal Dutch Airlines(2)	KL	254 8325
Korean Air(1)	KE	235 9220
Kuwait Airways(2)	KU	535 2337
Lao Aviation(1)	QV	236 9821
Lauda Air(2)	NG	233 2565
Lot-Polish(1)	LO	235 2223
LTU International Airways(2)	LT	561 3784
Lufthansa(2)	LH	264 2400
Malaysian Airlines(1)	MH	234 2985
Myanmar Airways(1)	UB	267 5078
Northwest Oriental(2)	NW	254 0781
Olympic Airways(1)	OA	237 6141
Pakistan International(1)	PK	234 2961
Philippine Airlines(1)	PR	233 2350
Qantas Airways(1)	QF	236 9193

On-Line Airlines	Airline Code	Phone
Royal Air Cambodge(1)	VJ	263 0565
Royal Bhutan Airlines(1)	KB	233 3810
(c/o Thai Airways)		
Royal Brunei Airlines(1)	BI	233 0056
Royal Jordanian(1)	RJ	236 0030
Royal Nepal(1)	RA	233 3921
Sabena(1)	SN	238 2201
SAS(1)	SK	260 0444
Saudi Arabian(2)	SV	236 9403
Singapore Airlines(1)	SQ	236 0440
South African Airways(1)	SA	254 8206
Swissair(2)	SR	233 2930
Tarom(1)	RO	253 1681
Thai Airways International(1)	TG	513 0121
Turkish Airlines(1)	TK	231 0300
United Airlines(2)	UA	253 0558
Uzbekistan Airways(2)	HY	233 6078
Varig Brazilian Airlines(1)	RG	231 3020
Vietnam Airlines(1)	VN	251 4242

In addition to the online airlines, there are those that are offline, ie they have offices in the city but do not fly into the country. These include: *Aerolineas Argentinas* (AR, ph 237 6146), *Air Canada* (AC, ph 233 5900), *Air Mauritius* (MK, ph 237 6145), *Air Mandalay* (6T, ph 381 0881), *Air Nuigini* (PX, ph 237 7251), *Air Seychelles* (HM, ph 237 6149), *Air Zaire* (QC, ph 235 4375), *Aloha Airlines* (AQ, ph 252 3520), *Alyemda Airlines* (DY, ph 255 3733), *American Airlines* (AA, ph 251 0806), *America West Airlines* (HP, ph 231 5635), *Ansett Australian Airlines* (AN, ph 254 4103), *British Midland* (BD, ph 237 6150), *Continental Airlines* (CO, ph 237 6145), *Iberia Airlines* (IB, ph 255 9966), *Ladeco Chilean Airlines* (UC, ph 237 6883), *Sempati Airlines* (SG, ph 254 4103), *Trans World Airlines* (TW, ph 233 7290), *Union de Transports Ariens* (UT, ph 233 7100), *US Air* (US, ph 237 6152) and *Yemenia Airways* (IY, ph 253 3063).

By Sea
Cruise ships frequently visit various destinations in Thailand. Cargo ships calling at Bangkok's Klong Toey port sometimes have passenger cabin facilities available.

Cruises also leave from Bangkok for Pattaya, Koh Chang and Koh Samui during May to October (ie out of the south-west monsoon period). From November to May, cruises leave from Phuket for the Andaman Sea.

With the opening of neighbouring Myanmar, it is easier to move between the two countries. For example, if you are in Ranong or Chumphon, you can spend 20 minutes and be in Kawthoung or Victoria Point, in Myanmar. From *Jansom Thara Resort*, on the Andaman Sea, you can travel by boat to Kawthoung without a passport. Phone the resort on (077) 821 611 for details.

Technically not the sea, but it is possible to cross 'water' to get into Myanmar, Lao PDR and Yunnan Province in China. From Chiang Khong you can cross the Mekong River (Mae Khong) into Lao PDR. One day trips across the river are possible. Border passes cost US$10 plus a passport, 3 photos and a valid Thai visa for re-entry. The Friendship Bridge links Nong Khai and The Deua in Lao PDR.

By Rail

There are train services connecting Thailand to Malaysia. These services include daily trains between Bangkok and Butterworth (opposite the island of Penang) and on to Kuala Lumpur and Singapore. Trains also go from Bangkok to Sungai Golok (Malaysia) via Hat Yai.

The Eastern & Oriental Express operates an exclusive return service from Bangkok to Singapore for wealthy train enthusiasts. Trains leave Singapore at 3.30pm and arrive in Bangkok two days later at 9am. Trains from Bangkok have the same departure and arrivals times. Fares range from B31,000 for sleeper compartments through to B81,000 for a Presidential Suite. This includes all meals and accommodation in opulent surroundings. It stops at Kuala Lumpur, Penang (Butterworth), Hat Yai, Surat Thani and Hua Hin on the way. Phone 216 0020, fax 253 2960 for more details.

Although closed at the present moment, the train line to Cambodia, via Aranyaprathet, will eventually open and enable tourists to travel through eastern Thailand into Cambodia.

By Road

With the opening of Myanmar, Lao PDR and Cambodia, there

are many more possibilities for travel into and out of Thailand.

Overland travel into Cambodia is still considered too dangerous due to Khmer Rouge activities in some border areas. As security improves, one may be able to cross at Aranyaprathet, Khao Ta Thong and Khao Phra Viharn (the latter, to see a famous Angkorian temple). Imperative to check first.

To travel overland into Myanmar, cross from Mae Sai into Tachilek for US$5. Sangklaburi-Three Pagodas Pass-Payathonzu, 225km north of Kanchanaburi, has always been a trading centre and it is now accessible to foreigners. The procedure is for visitors surrender their passport to the Thai officials and hand over B130 to the Myanmar officials. These journeys can only be done on a daily basis.

From Malaysia there are several roads leading into Southern Thailand. These include Padang Besar, Keroh-Betong Road, Changlun-Sadao, Wang Kelian-Satun, the new north-south highway border crossing (Bukit Kayu Hitam), Tak Bai (Ban Taba)-Kampung Pengkalan Kubor and Sungai Golok to Rantau Panjang. Gates at most crossings are open from 6am to 8pm. Some, however, close at 7pm. Thai and Malaysian officials are monitoring the need to keep the crossings open all day.

If you intend travelling by road throughout Thailand, statistics indicate that people on motor cycles, bikes and cars have a greater risk of accident than other forms of transportation. Take care and think seriously about taking out travel insurance.

By Bus
Access is similar to those listed above under *By Road*. Scheduled coach services connect Thailand with Malaysia and more recently Lao PDR. *VIP Buses* operate air-conditioned buses from Bangkok to Vientiene for B600. There are currently no services to Cambodia or Myanmar.

Package Tours
Most airlines operating into Thailand offer package tours that include airfares, accommodation, sightseeing and some meals. Some operators combine Thailand with other popular Asian destinations. As Indochina opens up some operators are combining Thailand with these neighbouring destinations. Packages often represent good value as savings obtained by the

airlines and large travel wholesalers are passed onto travellers.

Tourist Information

The Tourism Authority of Thailand (TAT) has its head office at 372 Bamrung Muang Road, Bangkok, ph 226 0060, fax 224 6221, and a counter at Bangkok International Airport. They also have offices throughout the country which are listed separately under the various destinations. The Tourist Assistance Centre can be contacted on 282 8129. The TAT has many brochures and staff to handle enquiries. A few overseas offices are listed to obtain information prior to travelling. There are offices in Hong Kong, Taipei, Seoul, Tokyo, Osaka, Fukuoka, Frankfurt, Paris, Rome and Chicago as well.

Australia. 12th Floor, Royal Exchange Building, 56 Pitt Street, Sydney 2000, ph 9247 7549, fax 9251 2465.

Malaysia. c/o Royal Thai Embassy, 206 Jalan Ampang, Kuala Lumpur, ph 248 0958, fax 241 3002.

Singapore. c/o Royal Thai Embassy, 370 Orchard Road, Singapore 093, ph 235 7694, fax 733 5653.

United Kingdom, 49 Albemarle Street, London WIX 3FE, England, ph 499 7679, fax 629 5519.

U.S.A. 3440 Wilshire Boulevard, Suite 1101, Los Angeles CA 90010, ph 382 2353, fax 389 7544; and 5 World Trade Centre, Suite 2449, New York, NY 10048, ph 432 0433, fax 912 0920.

Accommodation

Thailand caters to all tastes, from the world's consistently best hotel, *The Oriental,* in Bangkok, to very rudimentary village hut accommodation with northern hilltribe people.

THA has member hotels throughout the country, and at their counter at Don Muang Airport they provide a booking service. Most large hotels are subject to a 10% service charge and an 11% government tax. Many also have peak season supplement charges. The *Thai Hotel's Association (THA)* is compiling a directory of environmentally-friendly hotels for distribution to international travel organisations.

If you are staying in real budget accommodation you may have to supply your own towel, soap and toilet paper. Small chamois-type towels are good to carry. A sleeping sheet is recommended for hilltribe trekking and budget accommodation where cleanliness may not be satisfactory. A sleeping mat may also be a good idea.

In this guide, various types of accommodation have been listed in each regional section. In the more developed tourist destinations the information listed is quite detailed but in smaller locations only the phone number and tariff are included. I have offered a selection that caters to most budgets.

Local Transport

Air

There are two main companies operating domestic services, *Thai Airways* and *Bangkok Airways*.

Thai Airways flies domestically to Hat Yai, Nakhon Si Thammarat, Narathiwat, Phuket, Surat Thani, Trang, Chiang Mai, Chiang Rai, Lampang, Phrae, Phitsanulok, Nan, Mae Hong Son, Mae Sot, Khon Kaen, Nakhon Ratchasima, Sakon Nakhon, Nakhon Phanom, Ubon Ratchathani and Udon Thani. Departure tax on domestic flights is B30.

Bangkok Airways, Queen Sirikit National Convention Centre, New Rajjadapisek Road, Klong Toey, ph 229 3456, fax 229 3454, operates services from Bangkok to and from Ranong, Koh Samui and Hua Hin. It also flies from Koh Samui to Phuket and Koh Samui to U-Tapao. *Bangkok Airways* charge B100 to and from Koh Samui.

Thai Airways has a policy of fining passengers who do not show up for departures. Passengers who miss a flight without informing the airline three hours before departure, will be fined 10% of the airfare. This means more flights will depart full rather than be half-empty because of 'no shows'. It also means you do not have to reconfirm tickets. Counters close 30 minutes before departure and stand-by fares are available after this.

Charter helicopter services also operate from Don Muang to the city and other destinations. The *Riverside City Shopping Centre* for instance, has a heliport for the nearby *Royal Orchid Sheraton Hotel* and presumably not for the shops.

Rail

The train system of about 4500km is both extensive and efficient.

There are three classes, 1st, 2nd and 3rd. There are Rapid, Express, Special Express and normal trains. Sleeping births are sold as upper and lower; lower being the more expensive as it is slightly bigger. They are further divided into air conditioned and non-air conditioned. The fare is calculated according to all the above categories, the most expensive being 1st Class, Special Express sleeper with air conditioning. Tickets can be purchased at any rail station but best done at Bangkok's Hualamphong Station Central Booking Office, ph 223 7010. Tickets can be purchased in advance and this is recommended for holiday periods when the trains are usually quite full. Travel agents also book trains but will add on a service fee of about B100. This may not be such a bad idea, considering Bangkok's traffic and the time involved in obtaining tickets from the station.

If you have booked a sleeper, your first concern when you get on a train is, where is the sleeping berth? Don't be concerned, you are probably in the right carriage, but check anyhow. When the time comes in the early evening, the attendant will come along and magically convert your seat to a sleeper. Thai trains are very clean and comfortable. One advantage in booking a sleeper is that your accommodation and travel are combined, providing a cheap way to travel. The only thing missing is a shower in the morning. While trains are slower than buses they are certainly more comfortable and are my preferred way of getting around Thailand if I am not in a hurry.

Food is reasonably good on most long distance trains although it is not as good as it once was. In addition to the food sellers who move through the train, most long distance trains serve meals. This process usually involves filling in a form and having the food arrive at your designated time.

Bus

A modern highway system reaches most parts of the country. Domestic coach services offer fast means of travel. There are different terminals for different locations in the country. For information on buses call the following numbers: East, ph 390 130; North and North-East, ph 272 029; and South, ph 435 1199.

The Southern Bus Station is located on Charansanitwongse Road, ph 435 1200 (AC) and 435 5018 (regular). The Eastern Bus Station is situated at Soi 63, Sukhumvit Road. The North-East

Bus Terminal is being relocated. A temporary one is under construction on Kamphaengphet 11 Road, near Chatuchak Park (and the *Weekend Markets*). The temporary terminal will, for the first time, separate buses and passenger facilities by having two levels. It will be 'temporary' for 15 years. Buses for northern Thailand will continue to use Mor Chit Terminal.

Food and drinks are never a problem on buses as food sellers leap onto every bus at major depots.

Local buses in rural areas can get incredibly crowded. The best seats are near the back door because there is additional leg room. However, these areas may also become jammed with passengers. Watch your head getting up, tall people are not adequately accommodated. On long distance buses be prepared to watch loud and often violent videos.

Car

In order to hire a car, visitors must have a valid International Driving Licence. However, in many cases your national licence will suffice. Most road signs are in Thai and English so driving is not difficult. Officially, traffic drives on the left hand side of the road but some drivers may leave you guessing about this. Coaches and trucks overtaking on blind corners are, unfortunately, not an uncommon sight.

Maps are freely available and are often supplied by the rental company. You need to know that the capital of most provinces has the same name as the province, which can be a bit confusing when first reading a map. Premium and lead-free petrol are available everywhere and expect to pay about B98/litre. Rental agencies are found throughout the country at either airports or major hotels. You are best to check in Bangkok at the head offices of these companies to find out the nearest regional agent. The major international networks and their Bangkok offices are: *Avis,* ph 255 5300'; and *Hertz,* ph 391 0461. Others include: *Dollar Car Rent,* ph 233 0848; *Krung Thai Car Rent,* ph 246 1525; and *VIP Tours,* ph 251 4702.

Visitors should be warned that the majority of vehicle rental agencies do not carry insurance. Hire contracts with many operators make it clear the customer is liable for any damage to the vehicle, or for any injuries arising from an accident. Read the fine print before you hire. In some resorts, hirers are expected to surrender their passports as surety against loss or damage. This could present problems so you may want to negotiate to leave something else that isn't so important. All car owners are supposed to have third party insurance so if you intend driving in the country for some time, make sure you have such cover.

Taxi

Thai taxi drivers were once great rip-off merchants who fleeced innocent travellers. Now Bangkok taxis, especially, provide meters and fares are set. They are also very clean and most are air-conditioned. Many hotels provide limousine services at rates substantially higher than taxis.

In the rural districts, *songthaews,* or covered pick-up trucks (mostly *Isuzu*) operate as taxis. Bench seats along the sides and middle of the pick-up provide seating for anything up to 20 passengers. People also stand at the back although it is supposedly illegal to hang out the back or stand on the back steps. There isn't much headroom and the diesel fumes can be overpowering. Many trekking companies operating in the north will use these vehicles.

Tuk Tuk and Motor Bikes

Samlors or *tuk tuk* (named after the noise they make) are three-wheel motor bikes with a cabin that can hold between one and five people. They are very noisy and smelly, but are an exciting way to zip through the traffic. Now that taxis exist in the cities, *tuk tuks* have a bit of competition. Negotiate a reasonable fare that should be lower than a taxi fare because of the relative discomfort.

Boats

Longtail boats (*rua hang yao*) use the *klongs* and many of the rivers in the country. These boats operate with what appears to be a car motor mounted at the back of a long narrow boat. A long drive shaft with a propeller extends from the motor. They are incredibly noisy but provide the fastest means of water transport. Many of Bangkok's *klongs* are serviced by these boats. The Chao Phraya river is full of boats zig-zagging across its wide expanse. Some rivers in northern Thailand and Kanchanaburi are serviced by longtails. They are also common sights in coastal destinations like Krabi.

River cruising and rafting is popular on some rivers especially the Chao Phraya. The *Mekhala*, an old teak rice barge, is one such boat, ph (03) 256 7168 or fax (03) 256 7172, for details.

Food and Drinks

Food

This probably doesn't come as a surprise, but Thailand is the best place in the world to try Thai food. Regardless of how good your local Thai restaurant is back home, the real thing is far better. However, don't be too disappointed if your Thai hosts take you to *McDonald's* when you dine out. Thais have taken to Western fast foods with a passion. There are more fast varieties here than probably anywhere else in the world. Maybe this is an expression for the Thais that 'we have made it'.

Like every international city, a wide variety of food is available. Such food is also common in the major tourist destinations. It remains a mystery why anyone would choose fondue or *Wiener Schnitzel* when there is so much fine local food in Thailand. Fortunately, cheap but good Thai food is available everywhere. Hygiene is normally good in most locations even roadside stalls where most Thais eat. The food is cheapest here and usually the best. Sharing meals is also a Thai tradition and many tourists will have such an opportunity while in the country. Food is placed on the table for everybody to enjoy; individual serves are unusual and not part of Thai eating habits. There is a Thai expression, *khrob khrua* which, in a literal sense, means that anyone who shares food from the same kitchen, is part of the family.

Unlike their Asian neighbours, spoon and forks are commonly used although chopsticks are available for many noodle dishes. The spoon is held in the right hand and food is pushed onto it with the fork. Ingredients in most dishes are cut into bite-size pieces thus avoiding the need for knives. In the south, some people eat with their hand; the right one only.

Rice is the staple and is usually consumed with each meal, even breakfast, where *kao tom* is common. The main meal is the evening meal and several dishes accompany the rice. In a formal dinner, there will be a balance with certain ingredients complementing others. Such a meal may include five or six dishes of curry, soup, omelette, vegetables, fish and meat. In a restaurant, the dishes may be served in any order. If you require something first, you should specify this, if you can. Often you will have to ask for rice, usually steamed or *kao plow.*

Many people think Thai food is just hot because of the abundance of chili or *prik.* This assessment does a disservice to the many fine cooks of Thailand. Thai food is a delicate blend of many different spices. If you do not like your food hot you should ask to reduce the amount of chilli. Other spices and ingredients that are integral to Thai cooking include lemongrass, peanuts, coriander, coconut milk, ginger, basil, garlic, mint, lemon leaves and fish sauce (*nam pla*). Many meats are eaten; chicken, pork and beef, as well as seafoods. In Muslim parts of the country or restaurants, there is no pork on the menu.

Some common dishes include: beef curry in peanut sauce (*kaeng matsaman*), hot and sour soup (*tom yam*), pork omelette (*khai chieo mu sap*), fried rice (*khao phat*), fried chilli chicken (*kai phat phrik*), fried fish (*pla thot*), fried chicken (*kai yang*), and wonton soup (*kieo nam*).

Desserts, based upon eggs, mung beans, lotus seeds, cassava root and coconuts, are delicious. Local ice cream is also good with local flavours of sweet corn, coconut and durian.

There are many fruits available in Thailand, some familiar, some not. Try: guava (*farang*), jack fruit (*khanun*), longan (*lamyai*), rambutan (*ngo*), papaya (*malako*), mango (*mamuang*), mangosteen (*mangkhut*), pineapple (*sapparot*), and durian (*thurian*).

Drinks

Every conceivable brand of soft drink is available in Thailand. *Coke* is often sold as what looks like *'Tan'* in Thai. This must be one of the few markets in the world where *Coke* has a local spelling. Beer and Thai whisky are freely available throughout the country. According to an *Asiaweek* survey in 1995, Thai's love their alcohol. An estimated 32 million litres are consumed per annum, making it the fifth highest in the world. Beer brands includes *Singha, Kloster, Chang, Amarit* and *Khun Phaen* (found in the north-east only). *Singha Gold* has a lower alcohol content. *Carlsberg* (from Denmark, but made under license in Asia) and *Fosters* (Australia) are foreign beers seen in some of the tourist resorts. Other foreign beers are available in large city department stores. Thailand is also famous for its rice whisky. This bears no resemblance to Scotch whisky but is worth trying. It is mostly drunk with soda and ice. Thai's will love you for trying and drinking it. There are several brands, *Mekong* being the best known. In the hills of northern Thailand a white 'jungle juice' is distilled locally from rice. Try it if you are game.

Less fiery drinks include plain water (*nam plao*), ice (*nam khaeng*), hot water (*nam rawn*), tea (*cha*), milk coffee (*kafay ron*), iced coffee (*kafay yen*), and milk (*nom*).

Entertainment and Arts

Museums

The Department of Fine Arts operates 36 museums throughout the country, including five in Bangkok. They are open Wed-Sun, 9am-4pm. The same department is responsible for 20 significant cultural monuments, too. In 1992, several sites were placed on the prestigious UNESCO World Heritage Sites list as cultural features important to all people. These included Si Satchanalai Kamphaeng Phet Historical Park in Sukothai, Phra Nakhon Si Ayutthaya Historical Park, and Ban Chiang Archaeological Site in north-east Thailand.

Dance

Thai drama and dance in their classical forms are indivisible. The origins of dance are from India but they have been refined by the Thais. The dance is slow and graceful (neighbouring Khmers however, argue theirs is more refined). During dance performances the finger tips express what silent lips do not. Performances are accompanied by a small orchestra.

Shadow Puppets

Dance figures cut from buffalo hide are manipulated in front of a backlit screen to give a shadow effect. The theatre is called *nang yai* and stories relate to the *Ramakien*, the Thai *Ramayana*. Puppets are sold in many markets for tourists.

Music

Classical Thai music uses the diatonic music scale and, to many, it sounds like unrelated sounds and tones. To the trained and initiated, this is not the case. There are four types of instruments, those of drawing, plucking, percussion and woodwind, in a classic *phipat* orchestra. Other orchestra forms include *mahori* (string instruments) and *krung sai* (a rural orchestra with strings and wind instruments). Music accompanies drama, religious ceremonies and festivals.

Today, visitors to Thailand will be assaulted by music wherever they go. It seems many Thais feel lost without half a million decibels of sound. Sometimes when you enter a restaurant or taxi this wall of sound will be put on for your benefit, perhaps to reassure you that they have all modern facilities. If you can be heard over the noise, you can ask to have it turned down or off. Thais only want to please, they are not offended if you ask.

Nationwide, nightclubs, discos, bars, clubs and cinemas lure people out for a good time. Massage parlours attract people for a variety of other pursuits. Thai English-language newspapers carry daily listings of entertainment events such as cinema programs. Complimentary, *What's On*-style magazines (*Metro* is one example) are available in large hotels in major tourist areas.

What to Take

Some things to include are: an open mind, first aid kit, prescription drugs (*see section on Health and Safety*), mosquito net, penknife, suntan lotion, insect repellent, film (not all are freely available in the country, *see section on Photography*), camera, a sleeping sheet and mat if you are trekking, hat, umbrella (wet season), spare camera batteries, passport photos, torch, sanitary supplies, reading materials, swimmers, something other than shorts for temples, postcards of home to show people where you live and this guide book to make your visit more enjoyable.

Shopping

Thailand is a shopper's paradise with TAT estimating that 30% of all money spent by tourists is on shopping. Bargains can be found in local markets, department stores and exclusive designer boutiques.

Be a cautious when shopping as people who volunteer their services to help you shop may be given a commission by the shop owner. This is money you could have spent. Some people may offer to show you 'where the locals shop', which, they claim will be cheaper for you. It is up to you whether you go with these people, but if you do, expect to pay more. Some *tuk tuk* drivers will offer to show you the sights of Bangkok for a very cheap price. This 'tour' usually includes their friends' shops.

Gemstones and Jewellery (mainly rubies and sapphires, many of which come from neighbouring Cambodia) are popular purchases in Thailand. Gold settings are mostly 14 carat although all grades of gold are sold. Unless you know what you are doing you should restrict such purchases to reputable stores.

You may be offered deals to purchase such gemstones to make big profits by selling them back home. Ask yourself, if the profits are so good, why are these storeholders prepared to share the loot with me? Over 60% of complaints to the TAT are about gem scams. If you want to learn about gemstones attend the classes conducted by *Asian Institute of Gemological Sciences*, ph 541 4205, fax 541 4204.

Cotton products, especially from around Lamphun and the northern hilltribes are well worth buying. Most are now available from markets and tourist shops but you may still be able to buy a few old pieces from villagers if you go trekking in the north. Mudmee silk from the north-east is unique for its tie-dyed appearance.

Silk fabric from Thailand is considered some of the best in the world. It is produced around Chiang Mai (San Kamphaeng) and in Bangkok. Thai silk tends to be coarser than, say Chinese. Most silk centres in the country have established displays where the process of silk production from a caterpillar through to the finest fabric in the world, is explained. Most of the silk in Thailand is hand woven on one metre-wide looms that have been used for centuries.

Antiques and 'imitation' antiques are found in many handicraft shops throughout the country. There is a small problem in that antiques are not supposed to be exported despite what shopkeepers may tell you (it's a pity the authorities are not as strict about the theft and import of antiquities from neighbouring countries into Thailand). You may need a written assurance from the shop that you can return the goods if Customs refuse it for export. How you do this while waiting to board an international flight is a little confusing. Be cautious of many antiques as the Thais have perfected the art of ageing. As one retailer told me after I recognised the antique was fake, 'Same, same, only different.'!

There are many good locations for buying antiques, especially the north and Bangkok. The *River City Shopping Complex* near the Chao Phraya River is a good, but expensive start (it's a pity that many pieces for sale here come from Cambodia and, at one stage, must have been stolen).

Clothes are cheap within the country; the exception being real designer labels, which aren't cheap anywhere in the world. Thai rip-off designer labels are renowned and cheap (I still find it hard to believe *Gucci* ever designed gaudy gold-embossed T-shirts as the traders in Thai markets would have me believe). Buy them for the fun of it but don't think you will deceive the discerning fashion victim. Some shops sell samples of the real thing next to the rip-off; here you can tell the difference.

Rip-offs of all descriptions are available in the markets much to the concern of worldwide patent holders (purchasing rip-offs denies designers and musicians their royalties). Every so often the police get tough and round up a few rip-off watches for a ceremonial crushing for the international press. A few days later, the traders are back with new stock. If you want rip-off watches, computer software, sunglasses as well as clothes; Thailand's got it all.

Pewterware is made and sold in Thailand. Phuket was mined extensively for tin.

Silverware jewellery is high quality and a good buy in Thailand. The amount of silver carried by some hilltribe people is a sign of their wealth. Silver can be found in most markets and you can watch them make silver products on the outskirts of Chiang Mai. Hilltribe silver is usually heavy.

Lacquerware, or *lai rod nam,* is particularly striking in black on gold. Traditional designs include jungle scenes and repeated geometric designs.

Handicrafts from various parts of the country are available in many stores in Bangkok including the large department stores where prices are fixed. Chiang Mai is the preferred city if you are heading there. The days of picking up an old trinket painstakingly produced and sold for next to nothing, are over.

Many of the products are mass produced these days, but as a memento of your holiday, many are still worth buying. Embroidery, lacquerware, umbrellas, pottery, baskets and woodcarvings are good value.

Sightseeing

Today, there isn't much you can't see in Thailand. They have elephant theme parks, crocodile wrestling shows, traditional hilltribe dances, mini-worlds and cultural shows, etc. In this guide, the sights of specific destinations are listed for each area. Many sightseeing tours and events are things that can be seen in many parts of the world. In this book, I have concentrated on sights, events and festivals that are closer to the Thai culture and way of life.

Sports and Games

Golf, soccer, boxing, badminton, tennis, bowling and snooker figure prominently among international sports enjoyed by Thais. Indigenous games and sports include world famous Thai 'kick' boxing, takrao, kite-flying and boat racing. From December 9 to 17, 1995, Thailand hosted the SEA Games in Chiang Mai.

Sailing and Boat Racing

There are many destinations around the coast where boats can be chartered with a crew or without one (bareboat). Boat racing is featured in many country fairs which celebrate the end of the annual Buddhist Rains Retreat in October. The long, narrow, low-slung wooden boats are festooned with flowers and flags.

Diving

Access to both the Andaman Sea and the Gulf of Thailand ensure year round diving. The best time to visit the Andaman Sea is from November to March and in the Gulf, from February to May. Live aboard diving is possible in many destinations especially the Similan Islands which are some distance from the coast. Most coastal destinations have organisations conducting recognised dive lessons. You should allocate about seven days to learn to dive. Serious divers should consult *Diving Escapades in Thailand's Tropical Waters*, a comprehensive dive book on all sites in the country (*see section on Books, Films and Maps*).

Golf

In Asia it seems, anyone wanting to succeed must play golf. Thailand is no different. Golf courses are opening throughout the country to cater to visiting golfers and a growing number of locals. There are at least 175 courses with another 50 under construction. The smallest is a three-holer near the Cambodian border. Concerns have been expressed about the environmental problems associated with the expansion of golf courses.

Kite-Flying

Kites have been popular in Thailand since the 13th century for both recreation and warfare. In 1690, a governor quelled a rebellion by flying massive kites over a besieged city and bombing it into submission. Today, kite flying is either an individual pursuit or a competitive sport. During the hot months opposing teams fly male (*chula*) and female (*pakpao*) kites in a surrogate battle of the sexes. The small agile *pakpao* tries to fell the larger *chula* while the male kite tries to ensnare the female kite. Kites are a common site even in the back streets of cities. The tell tail signs of kites suspended from power lines indicates how widespread is the sport. Sanam Luang, near the Royal Palace in Bangkok is a good place to see and buy colourful kites.

Takrao

Traditionally, the game is played by a loosely formed circle of males who use their feet, knees, thighs, chests and shoulders to pass a woven, hollow rattan ball to each other. The aim is to keep the ball off the ground for as long as possible. A form of volley ball is also played using the same ball. The balls are on sale in markets and the game is a lot of fun if you want to try.

Thai Boxing

This type of boxing developed as a form of self-defence during the Ayutthaya period (1350 to 1767). Boxers are forbidden to bite, spit or wrestle, however, they may kick, shove, push and unrestrainedly use bare feet, legs, elbows and shoulders. Fists are the main form of attack or defence. Thai boxing is featured in Bangkok and tourist destinations such as Pattaya.

Photography

In many countries like Thailand, it is impolite to thrust cameras in people's faces. Unless you have a long lens and can take photos of people from a distance, it is polite to ask or indicate you would like to take their photo. My experience is that many Thais enjoy having their photograph taken. This is not always the case in the south, where people appear to be a little more sensitive to cameras. Sometimes Thais are too obliging and stop the activity you wish to photograph, to pose for you. You may consider offering some money for posing. Normally, I would not do this but as many people in rural areas are poor, a little money for their time may be appropriate. In well-touristed areas, you may not have a choice.

All Buddha images, no matter how big or small or in whatever state of disrepair, are sacred objects. Don't climb on them to take photos or have people pose on them.

Equipment

Take as much as you can carry as it is always the piece of equipment that you leave behind that is needed. Others argue that carrying too much equipment is a nuisance. The decision is yours. On many occasions you will need to carry your own baggage, so take what you can carry. While there is a loss in picture quality with many zoom lenses, they do save weight. A 35mm to 80mm zoom is handy. Longer lenses (eg 200mm) are good for taking people and distance shots. A small tripod will be useful in low light situations like the insides of *wats*. Alternatively, take a flash. A polarising filter (learn how to use it properly) is useful for Asian skies. Graduated blue and yellow filters (eg *Cokin* brand) will enhance grey and overcast skies. Bring spare batteries as you may run out at the most inappropriate time. Before leaving for Thailand, have your camera checked, especially the battery.

Bangkok is certainly not the cheapest place in the world to buy new or secondhand camera equipment; for example, if you are heading to Kuala Lumpur it is far cheaper there. However, every photographer needs to replace some equipment in an emergency and if so you should head to one of the following places in Bangkok: *Foto Hobby*, ph 252 2764; *Foto File*, ph 217 9426 or *Queen's Camera*, ph 252 7548. For camera repairs try *T.K. Camera Repair*, ph 253 3827.

Film

Choose between slide and print film based on how you use your photographs and the audience who will see them. It is expensive to obtain prints from slides but almost impossible to get good slides from prints. The light in Thailand is mostly good and film speed (ISO) selection need not be higher than 200ISO. The light in most places is best just after sunrise and just before sunset when it is low and usually golden. Midday light is intense in Asia and in many cases it is almost a waste of time taking photos. Many of us are in places at the wrong time so don't get too disappointed if your photos don't turn out as you hoped. Film is freely available in Thailand, however, the range is not always extensive. If you use special film, bring it with you. There are many processing shops around and the quality is usually good and cheaper than in the west.

All the photos in this book were taken on *Fuji Velvia* (50ISO) or *Provia* (100ISO), my favourite films for the skies of Asia.

Books, Films and Maps

There are many books on Thailand and Thai culture and there are many good places to buy these books. In Bangkok (the larger stores have branches throughout the country), look out for the following stores: *Bookazine Stores*, Bangkok, ph 231-0016; Pattaya, ph 038 710 472; *Asia Books*, ph 2527277; *D.K. Book House*, ph 252 6261; *The Bookseller*, ph 233 1717; and *Odeon*, ph 251 4476. There are several libraries in universities, embassies and institutions. Reference materials can be consulted at: the *British Council*, ph 252 6136; *Chulalongkorn University Library*, ph 215 4100; *National Library*, ph 281 5450; *Siam Society*, ph 258 3494; and the *National Museum Library*, ph 224 1333.

Further Reading

Fang, S. 1993. *Diving Escapades in Thailand's Tropical Seas, Your Underwater Guide*. SNP Publishers, Singapore. An excellent guide to most dive sites in the country.

Guelden, M. 1995. *Thailand: Into the Spirit World*. Times Editions, Singapore. A very good insight into the Thai views on religion from Buddhist, Hindu and animist perspectives.

Hewison, K. 1993. *Thailand.* Asia-Australia Briefing Papers, Vol 2 No 4, The Asia-Australia Institute, University of NSW, Australia. This is one of a series on Asian countries. Individual copies cost $A60. The book is essential reading for people interested in doing business in Thailand.

Hirsch, P. 1990. *Development Dilemmas in Rural Thailand.* Oxford University Press, Singapore. This is an excellent analysis of recent rural development in the country.

Hollinger, C. *Mai Pen Rai Means Never Mind.* Asia Books, Bangkok. Written by a long time expatriate woman, and details her often hilarious experiences, especially her deep love for her new home.

Hoskin, J. 1994. *The Supernatural in Thai Life.* The Tamarind Press, Bangkok. This small paperback delves into the darker side of Thai life with matters such as tattoos, fortune telling, spirits, animism and Buddhism, covered.

Hoskin, J. 1988. *Collins Illustrated Guide To Thailand.* Collins, London. A good, brief guide to the main features of the country.

Kemf, E. 1993. *The Law of the Mother: Protecting Indigenous Peoples in Protected Areas.* Sierra Club Books, San Francisco. There are good chapters on the Karen and Hmong hilltribe groups.

Lewis, P and E. 1984. *Peoples of the Golden Triangle.* Thames and Hudson, London. A detailed description of the hilltribes accompanied by excellent photos.

Lloyd, W. 1995. *Bangkok's Waterways: An Explorer's Handbook.* A very useful, illustrated guide to the waterways.

Piprell, C and Ashley Boyd. 1995. *Diving in Thailand.* Asia Books, Bangkok. Everything you need to know about Thailand's underwater world.

Smitthi, S. and E. Moore. 1993. *Palaces of the Gods, Khmer Art and Architecture in Thailand.* Asia Books, Bangkok. An authoritative work on the major Khmer architectural sites in Thailand which is well illustrated by Michael Freeman's photos.

Veran, G. 1979. *50 Trips Through Siam's Canals.* A good guide to people interested in seeing the country from a boat.

Warren, W. *Jim Thompson: The Legendary American.* Jim Thompson Thai Silk Company, Bangkok. This is the ultimate book on the legendary silk king.

Additional Reading and Maps

APA Maps. *Thailand 1:1.5 million scale* (includes city maps of Bangkok, Chiang Mai, Pattaya & Hat Yai).

Nancy Chandler's maps of Bangkok and Chiang Mai are unique for locating the obvious and the oddities.

Tour'n Guide Map, Bangkok Thailand, available for B50.

Bangkok Computer Guide, a desktop computerised map of the capital available in both Thai and English. It contains all the main streets, sois, and over 7000 landmarks, ph 250 1856.

Golf Courses of Thailand, available from 32 Golf, 25/1 Sukhumvit, Soi 31, ph 258 4604. Available for B500.

The monthly, *Bangkok Metro Magazine,* ph 679 8548, provides an excellent listing of events, cuisine, music, film, stage, art, literature and sport in the city. It costs B80 from newsstands.

Bangkok

People either love or hate Bangkok, there isn't much middle ground. Bangkok is known as the 'City of Angels'. Why?, nobody seems to know, because, a city of angels, it isn't. Some have less kindly, but more appropriately, called it a 'city of engines'. The name is derived from *bang* (meaning village) and *kok* (meaning plum-olive).

The Thais call the city *Krung Thep*, an abbreviation of its real name which has made the *Guinness Book of Records* as the world's longest place name, even longer than that place in Wales! The abridged translation is, 'jewelled city of the god Indra'. It was established in 1782 by King Rama I as the capital of Siam, as Thailand was then called. It has now spread over both sides of the alluvial floodplain of the mighty Chao Phraya River, which flows into the Gulf of Siam.

Bangkok is home to the respected Thai Royal Family, the seat of government, the administrative centre and the focal point for most of the country's commerce.

The city covers an area of 1565 km^2 and is located 14° north of the Equator.

How to Get There

Bangkok's Don Muang is Thailand's major international airport and the one most international travellers will use to enter the country (*see Travel Information chapter*). The Airport phone number is 535 1111, International Departure Information ph 535 1254. For domestic flights the airport phone number is 535 2081 and Information, 535 1253. There are now three terminals at the airport. There are two international terminals (1 and 2) and Domestic. If you are catching an international flight the terminals are about 100 metres apart so it is helpful to know from from what terminal one is departing. A second airport to be built at Nong Ngu Hao was planned but shelved in 1997. The existing airport at Don Muang can handle over 30 million passengers per year.

The current airport is 25 km from the city centre but this is better reflected in travelling time as the journey could take between 30 minutes and two hours depending on traffic and time of day. If you are travelling independently, you should allow between one to two hours; it is best to relax at the airport and catch your plane rather than fume in Bangkok traffic while missing your plane. If you have an organised transfer, you will be collected from your hotel at the appropriate time.

Both international and domestic arrivals and departures work very smoothly with 20 minutes being maximum to clear immigration and customs. 'Helpers' in uniformed jackets will assist you as you depart customs. Do not be suspicious of these officials, they are there to help. The airport has everything to facilitate travel and all signs are written clearly in English. You can arrange transport, accommodation and package tours from here. There are money exchanges, a post office, restaurants, left luggage counters, duty free shops, and airline counters for reconfirming or buying tickets. Buses or walkways connect international and domestic terminals.

Transfers to the city can be in *Thai Airways* limousines (from B500) and mini bus (B1,000 for charter of the whole bus), airport taxis (B250) or public taxis. The latter could be cheapest if you negotiate hard. You either pay at the counter and receive a slip with your destination which you hand to the driver, or you pay the driver when you arrive. Taxis will ask for an extra B30 toll for the freeway if they use it. Buses No 4, 10, 13 and 29 go to and from the city, but are probably best left to experienced budget travellers. Bus 10 goes to the Southern Bus Terminal, once again, only for the experienced. At a price of B16, though, it is the cheapest way. Once you leave the terminal you may be hassled by touts so pre-determine your journey and accommodation.

Departure tax for domestic flights is B30 for *Thai Airways* and *Bangkok Airways*. Koh Samui, which is privately owned, has a B100 departure tax. For international flights it is B200.

Tourist Information

The TAT Office is at 372 Bamrung Muang Road, Bangkok, ph

226 0060, fax 224 6221. It is open seven days per week, including public holidays. They have trained staff who efficiently handle phone and personal enquiries as well as distribute a range of brochures on every destination and on most topics relating to Thai life.

Accommodation

There is no shortage of accommodation in Bangkok and other large cities in Thailand. At the end of 1996, there were over 45,000 tourist beds in the capital (this figure doesn't include all the small backpacker places, either). The good news for travellers is that rates have dropped due to an oversupply.

Before booking accommodation in Bangkok, determine the purpose of your trip and then try to stay as close as possible to what you have come to see or do. Traffic is a major problem and the last thing you want to do is be caught up in it for the duration of your visit. If you are transiting to another destination try and stay as close to the airport as possible (unfortunately there isn't much choice). If you are shopping, stay near the shops, etc. My advice is to walk where possible, to as many destinations as you can. You will probably move as quickly as the traffic.

When arriving at the airport there is an accommodation counter. These people represent certain hotels and will not give information on those they don't. In some cases, they give selective information. Few cheap hotels are represented so there isn't much information on them. However, there are cheap hotels available, and for a more detailed list, consult TAT.

Following is a selection with prices for a double room per night, that should be used as a guide only. The telephone area code is 02.

Deluxe Hotels

Dusit Thani, 946 Rama IV Road, ph 236 0450, fax 236 6400. 533 AC rooms, IDD, satellite TV, pool, restaurants, bars, health club, business centre, disco, shops. From B5200.

Hilton International, 2 Witthayu Road, Nai Lert Park. ph 253 0123, fax 253 6509. 400 AC rooms, IDD, satellite TV, restaurants, bars, health club, pool, disco, shops. From B4400.

Grand Hyatt Erawan. 494 Ratchadamri Road, ph 254 1234, fax 253

5856. 408 AC rooms, IDD, satellite TV, pool, health club, business centre, restaurants (*Spasso's*), bars, disco, shops (adjacent to *Sogo*). From B5000.

Montien, 54 Surawongse Road, ph 234 8060, fax 236 5219. 496 AC rooms, IDD, satellite TV, restaurants (*Monti Brasserie, Jade Garden*), bars, pool, shops, business centre. From B4680.

Oriental, 48 Oriental Ave, New Road, ph 236 0400, fax 236 1937. 393 AC rooms, IDD, satellite TV, restaurants (*Normandie, China House, Lord Jim's, Ciao* & *Sala Rim Naam*), bars, health club, pool, exclusive shopping arcade, business centre. This is the best in town, if not the world as it consistently wins such awards. Wonderful location besides the Chao Phraya River and worth a visit if only to sit and watch people (dress appropriately or you won't be allowed in). From B6000.

Regent of Bangkok, 155 Ratchadamri Road, ph 251 6127, fax 253 9195. 415 AC rooms, IDD, satellite TV, restaurants (*Brasserie, Grill,* & *Spice Market*), bars, health club, pool, shops, business centre. This was originally the *Peninsula Hotel* and the lobby is based upon the famous *Peninsula* in Hong Kong. From B5885.

Royal Orchid Sheraton, 2 Captain Bush Lane, Si Phaya Road, ph 266 0123, fax 236 8320. 771 AC rooms, IDD, satellite TV, pool, restaurants, bars, health club, shops, business centre. It is located near antique stores in the *Riverside Centre.* All rooms have river views. From B6121.

Sheraton Grande Sukhumvit, 250 Sukhumvit Road, Klongtoey, ph 653 0333, fax 653 0408. 445 AC rooms, pool, IDD, satellite TV, compact disc player, restaurants (*Riva's, Rossini's,* & *The Sala*), health club and spa, business centre. From B6500.

Superior Hotels

Amari Airport Hotel, 333 Choet Wutthakat Road, Don Muang, ph 566 1020, fax 566 1941. 300 AC rooms, IDD, satellite TV, gym, pool, restaurants, shopping arcade (with an excellent bookshop) which is linked directly to the airport terminal. Between 8am and 6pm, they have three hour mini-stay rooms for B550 (single) and B600 (double) for passengers on a "walk in" basis (they can't be booked). From B4200.

Amari Watergate, 847 Petchburi Road, ph 653 9000, fax 653 9045. AC, IDD, satellite TV, pool, health club, business centre, big rooms, 24 hour coffee shop, five restaurants (Indian, Thai,

Chinese, Vietnamese & Japanese), and *Henry J. Bean's* American-style bar & grill. From B4680.

Indra Regent, 120/126 Ratchaprarop Road, ph 252 1111, fax 253 3849. 439 AC rooms, IDD, satellite TV, pool, restaurants, bars, health club, disco, shopping arcade, business centre. From B3413.

Landmark, 138 Sukhumvit Road, ph 254 0404, fax 253 4259. 415 AC rooms, IDD, satellite TV, restaurants (*Suri Sian, Kiku No Hana, Hibiscus* & *Rib Room* with a great view from the rooftop restaurants), bars, health club, business centre, shopping arcade. From B4826.

Le Meridien President, 135/26 Gaysorn Road (also fronts onto Sukhumvit Road), ph 253 0444, fax 253 7565. 387 AC rooms, IDD, satellite TV, restaurants, bars, pool, health club, shops. From B3531.

Monarch Lee Gardens, 188 Silom Road, ph 238 1991, fax 238 1999. 430 AC rooms, IDD, satellite TV, restaurants (including the *Tijing* with a great view of the city from its 38th floor), bars, pool, health club, business centre, shops. From B4000.

Siam Intercontinental, 967 Rama 1 Road, ph 253 0355, fax 253 2275. 400 AC rooms, IDD, satellite TV, restaurants, bars, health club, pool, shops, business centre. From B5179.

Sukothai, 13/3 Sathorn Tai Road, ph 259 2896, fax 287 4980. 190 AC rooms, IDD, satellite TV, restaurants, bars, health club, pool, shops, business centre. From B5297.

Standard Hotels

Asia, 296 Phaya Thai Road, ph 215 0808, fax 215 4360. 640 AC rooms, IDD, satellite TV, restaurants, bars, health club, disco, business centre, shops. Popular with large tour groups and well located to *Siam Square.* From B2600.

Bangkok Palace, 1091/336 New Petchaburi Road, ph 253 0510, fax 253 3359. 692 AC rooms, IDD, satellite TV, restaurants, bar, gym, pool, disco, shops, business centre. From B2708.

Collins International House (YMCA), 27 Sathon Thai Road, ph 287 1900, fax 287 1996. 258 AC rooms, IDD, satellite TV, restaurant, gym, pool, shops, business centre. From B1060.

Jim's Lodge, 125/7 Soi Ruamrudi, Wireless Road, ph 255 3100, fax 253 8492. 75 AC rooms with a coffee shop. From B2000.

Rex, 762/1 Sukhumvit Soi 32, ph 255 3100, fax 258 6635. 131 AC rooms, restaurant, bar, pool, shops. From B1755.

Budget Hotels

Bangkok Youth Hostel, 25/2 Phitsanulok Road, See Soa Theves, Dusit, ph 282 0950. Dormitory and rooms with fan, private shower/toilet, reading room, cafeteria. From B50.

City Lodge 1, 8/7 Soi 19, Sukhumvit Road, ph 254 4783, fax 255 7340. 35 rooms, restaurant, bar, disco. From B1000. There is also a *City Lodge 11*, at Soi 9, that offers similar facilities.

Grace, 12 Soi 3 Sukhumvit Road, ph 253 0651, fax 253 0680. 542 AC rooms, restaurant, bar, gym, pool, disco, shops, business centre. From B766.

Prince, 1537/1 New Petchaburi Road, ph 251 6171, fax 251 3318. 210 AC rooms, restaurant, bar, pool, shops. From B660.

Reno, 40 Soi Kasemsan 1, Rama 1 Road, ph 215 0026, fax 215 3430. 65 AC rooms and a coffee shop. From B550.

YMCA, 27 South Sathorn Road, ph 286 1936. 58 rooms and cottages, restaurant, pool, sporting facilities. From B500.

Guest Houses

Khao San Road near Democracy Monument is the mecca for those on a budget. Apart from guest houses, restaurants, discos and associated activities, there is a thriving market in fake ID cards; what is that spurs backpackers to take on another identity?

A One Inn, 13-15 Soi Kasemsan 1, Rama 1 Road, ph 216 4770, fax 216 4771. 15 AC rooms and a small restaurant. Friendly staff. From B400.

Ploy, 2/2 Khaosan Road, ph 282 1025. 40 rooms from B100.

We-Train, 501/1, Moo 3, Dechatungka Road, Don Muang, ph 566 2288, fax 566 3481. 27 AC rooms with bathrooms plus a big dormitory. This is a good one for those who need to stay overnight at the airport, although it's difficult to find. It's a little like a *YMCA* as they have rules. There is a cafeteria, pool, sauna, etc. Compared to other places near the airport it is good value. From B440.

Local Transport

Getting around Bangkok is not meant to be easy. The traffic is a constant topic of discussion in the city. Every day the newspapers have something devoted to it. The latest government proposals are for three mass transit solutions; urban highways and a mass transit system featuring elevated electric trains. Fears that Bangkok will lose its competitive business edge as a regional hub are coming closer to fruition every day. While the talks continue, more cars are added to the already jammed roads. As suggested before, work out what you want to do in Bangkok (business, sightseeing, shopping, etc) and then select a location that best suits your needs.

Bus

The good news is, Bangkok is well served by buses (including mini and extended 'bendy' buses). The bad news is, they get caught in jams like every other vehicle. At least you can read or sleep on a bus. Short journeys on AC buses cost B6 and non-AC, B3.50. The system works well with the AC buses less crowded, and more pleasant to ride. Bus users will need a copy of the bus routes and map. The *Tour'n Guide Map, Bangkok Thailand,* costs B50 from most guesthouses in Bangkok. It is invaluable.

Taxi

There are taxis and there are 'taxis'. Official taxis have a sign 'taxi meter' on the roof. The fares are fixed at B35 for the first two kilometres. Longer journeys are based upon distance and time (the meters are calculated for speeds of six km/hour, such are traffic jams in the city). The meter reads the time you are in the taxi, distance travelled, and the fare. It's quite simple and one of the best ways to get around the city. One problem is that many drivers, on spotting a tourist, will ask a fixed price claiming the meter is broken. Getting a taxi from Patpong Road is often difficult for these reasons. You should insist upon the meter being used or get out because you will be ripped-off, for sure. Older taxis have no meter and you determine the fare with the driver before you travel. Their initial price is usually ridiculously expensive; negotiate down. Cars masquerading as taxis often operate outside guesthouses. If the fare is low enough they are also a good way of travelling.

Car

Driving is probably best left to the experts or the masochists. The *Yellow Pages* of the Bangkok phone directory lists many car rental agencies (*see Local Transport section in Travel Information chapter*). The main streets of Bangkok are intersected by smaller streets which are called *sois*. Side streets going off a main street are often named as *sois* of the main street. Thus, Sukhumvit, Soi 16, is the 16th side street going of Sukhumvit Street, and it lies between Sukhumvit Soi 14 and Sukhumvit Soi 18. Odd numbers are on one side of the street and even on the other.

Tuk Tuks and Motorbikes

Tuk tuks are an exciting and efficient way to get through the traffic. They are a little smelly and dirty but then, so is Bangkok. Fares should start at about B40 for short trips, but you will have to negotiate hard to get this. Motor bikes also operate in the big cities especially at main exits from the main roads. They are meant for short distances. All the drivers have numbers attached to their backs.

Rail

There are few train connections within the city. Irregular trains go to the airport and for B20, are cheaper than a taxi. For the inconvenience of getting to Hualamphong Station in Bangkok, it is however, not recommended. If you are arriving at Bangkok Airport and then travelling to the country by train, Don Muang train station connects with most rail routes.

Longtail Boats (rua hang yao) and Ferries

The only way to see some parts of city is from a boat. Being a floodplain delta the city is flat and crossed by streams that are known as *klongs* or canals. The Chao Phraya River is the largest of the streams, and the most exciting no matter what the time of day. Many of the city's tourist attractions and sights line the river bank. The *Chao Phraya Express boats* move up and down the river with their low, sleek cabins. Users of these boats need to take notice of the word 'express' as boarding and getting off is rapid with most passengers jumping as quickly as possible. If you hesitate you will find yourself preparing to be a little quicker for the next ferry. They operate during daylight hours and cost B6. While they travel the length of the river, smaller ferries go across the river. It is an adventure working it all out but someone will help and guide you if you get lost.

Noisy longtail boats can also be hired along the river. Many tourists use them to go on canal cruises. Other larger longtail boats operate regular services along the smaller klongs. Many of these are canals of black liquid; don't fall in! Longboats operating on the klongs have plastic drop down sides to keep the black muck and rain out.

Eating Out

Some eat to live, others live to eat. Most Thais fall into the latter which makes for an exciting time for gourmets. Many fine restaurants are located in hotels or shopping malls. This often means service and government charges are added, making for a more expensive meal. Cheap food is available on virtually every street corner and is as good as in hotel restaurants, lacking only the ambience, or is it? Some would argue that the ambience of streetlife is better than in air conditioned premises. Street food is more traditionally Thai and it is here you will learn more about the culture. If you are convinced the premises are hygienic, try eating where the locals do but learn a little Thai first so that you can safely order your food. It is difficult to recommend street stalls as they are found all over the city and many come and go.

The following restaurants fall into the mid to higher price brackets but do not assume that these are the only places to eat. Explore the streets and you will find many that equal this list. Don't be disappointed if all you see in shopping malls are American-style fast food chains.

In addition to thousands of Thai restaurants and stalls, Bangkok offers a wealth of international food including Asian regional specialities. Isan (from the north-east) and northern food is found in many parts of Bangkok, however, southern Thai food is less widely distributed.

Japanese and Asian Restaurants

Arirang House (Korean), 106 Silom Road, ph 234 1096.
Bali (Indonesian), 15/3 Soi Ruam Rudi, Ploenchit Rd, ph 250 0711.
Bane Lao (Lao), 49 Sukhumvit Rd, Soi 36, ph 258 6096. Kobune, World Trade Centre/Fortune Town and Mah Boon Krong Centre.
Le Dalat (Vietnamese), 47/1 Sukhumvit Rd, Soi 23, ph 258 4192.
Moghul Room (Indian), 1/16 Sukhumvit Rd, Soi 11, ph 253 6989.
Silk Road (Japanese), 2/1 Sukhumvit Road, Soi 24, ph 258 8623.

Meals With A View

The Skylounge (*Baiyoke Hotel* on the 43rd floor, ph 253 0362); *Normandie* (*Oriental Hotel,* for those with a passion for French food, Chao Phraya River views, and have a wallet to match it); *Rotunda* (*Narai Hotel,* revolving restaurant); *Tiara Room* (*Dusit Thani Hotel,* ph 236 0450, overlooks Lumpini Park); the new restaurant on top of the *Sofitel Riverside Hotel* has spectacular views of the river; *Bar B Q* on top of the *Riverside City Shopping Centre* has good views of the Chao Phraya River.

Thai Restaurants with Thai Classical Dance

Baan Thai, 7 Soi 32, Sukhumvit Road, ph 258 5403. *Piman Thai Theatre,* 46 Sukhumvit, Soi 49, ph 258 7866 (show from 8.45-9.30pm) and *Silom Village Trade Centre,* 286 Silom Road, ph 235 8760 (show starts at 8pm).

Thai Restaurants

Ban-Chiang, Soi Sriviang, ph 236 7045. Cheap food, located near Silom Road.

Bussaracum, 35 Soi Pipat 2, Convent Road, ph 235 8915. Difficult to find but many consider it to be one of the best in the city.

Cabbages and Condoms, 10 Sukhumvit Road, Soi 12, ph 252 7349. Yes, you read it correctly. Established by Mechai Veravaidya and *OXFAM* to raise awareness about AIDS and safe sex. Oddity that attracts westerners. Funds raised from the restaurant and attached shop go to AIDS awareness.

Lemon Grass, 5/1 Sukhumvit, Soi 24, ph 258 8637, a little upmarket but with a big reputation.

Mangkoode, 41 Soi 8, Sukhumvit Road, ph 253 2758. This stylish restaurant serves exotic Thai dishes; try the parmelo salad and one of the best coconut ice creams in the city.

Patara (ph 656 1104) on level 3 of Gaysorn Plaza, serves authentic Thai dishes.

Sanuk Neuk, 397/1 Sukhumvit Road, Soi 55, ph 493 5590.

Seafood Restaurant ('if it swims, we have it'), used to be on Sukhumvit Road but has moved to 89 Soi 24, Sukhumvit Road; this supermarket-style restaurant is a Bangkok institution.

Silom Village, on Silom Road, has a selection of fine restaurants.

Thanying Princess (ph 255 9838) in the *World Trade Centre* and its associated restaurant on Silom Road, offer genuine Royal Thai cuisine at a reasonable price.

The Food Centre, Mah Boon Krong Centre, has a wide selection of food that is at a fixed price and paid for by buying coupons.

Tum Nak Thai, 131 Rachadapisek Road, ph 274 6420. According to the *Guinness Book of Records,* this is the world's largest restaurant with roller-skating waiters to serve the customers. It has 3000 seats, covers an area of 4ha, has a 250 dish menu and 1000 staff. Traditional dances are performed from 8pm to 9.30pm.

Vegetarian Restaurants

Whole Earth, 93/3 Soi Langsuan, Ploenchit Road, ph 252 5574, not so cheap but a long time favourite.

You Sue Vegetarian, 241 Rama IV Road, ph 214 2801.

Western Restaurants

Al Centro (Italian), Queen Sirikit National Convention Centre, New Ratchadapisek Road, ph 229 3000.

Alfredo (Italian), Asoke Tower, 211 Sukhumvit Rd, ph 258 3909.

Angelini (fusion) in the *Shangri-la Hotel* ph 236 7777.

Angus Steak House, 595/11 Sukhumvit Soi 33/1, ph 259 4444 (a favourite with meat-eaters).

Bierstube (German), 569 Sukhumvit Road, ph 258 9303.

California Pizza (Pizza), Silom Complex, Silom Road, ph 233 2151.

El Gordo's (Mexican), Silom Road, Soi 8, ph 234 5470.

Ma Maison (French), Hilton Hotel, Wireless Road, ph 253 0123.

Planet Hollywood (USA), Gaysorn Plaza, 999 Ploechit Rd, ph 656 1358.

Tapas (Spanish), 114/17 Silom Road, Soi 4, ph 234 4737.

For something different to do in Bangkok, attending the *Oriental Hotel Cooking School* (ph 437 3080) could enable you to impress at your next dinner party. There are classes five days per week at B2500/day. You can stay at the hotel, attend five days of classes and go on tours of the city for a cool US$2330/person.

The *YMCA* (ph 286 2329) may not impress many people, but the cooking school there is also good and a lot cheaper at B3000 for a seven day course.

The *Oriental* is a must for followers of great hotels. Afternoon tea in the *Author's Lounge* and a meal or drink on the *Riverside Terrace,* are two of Bangkok's culinary indulgences.

Entertainment

Bangkok's nightlife and entertainment are legendary not only throughout the region but probably the world. There are few activities that are not available in the city, both legal and illegal. In many ways, it is a 'man's' town, although this image is slowly changing for the better. Places come and go, so check a magazine like *Metro* when in Bangkok to see what is currently the hottest place in town.

Night Clubs and Bars

Bangkok has it all from Go Go Clubs (hard to believe, but it seems the 70s live on in Bangkok), karaoke lounges, American theme nightclubs, strip joints, discos, techno clubs, jazz clubs and bars.

Patpong Road, off Silom Road, is the centre of Bangkok's girlie bars. You can see it all here, if you choose. There are suggestions that this industry is based upon forced prostitution for many young women.

Henry J. Bean's, an American 50s style grill, bar and night spot is located in the *Amari Watergate Hotel* (ph 653 9000). *Spasso*, in the *Grand Hyatt Erawan Hotel* (ph 254 1234), changes from an Italian restaurant to a smart dance club with live music from 10.30pm to 1.30am. Along similar lines is *Hard Rock Café* (ph 251 0792) in Siam Square. Here there is the universal music theme, American burgers, souvenir shop (to prove you were there) and live music in the evening. *Planet Hollywood*, another American theme restaurant is located in the *Gaysorn Plaza*.

Other music venues include several bars in Soi Cowboy (off Sukhumvit Road at Soi 23); *Cowboy 2* and *Five Star*. *Nasa Spacedrome* (999 Ramkamhaeng Road, ph 314 6530) is the city's most established disco but has been taken over by the very young. *Narcissus* on Sukhumvit, Soi 23, is similar.

Good, live jazz each night at *Brown Sugar* (231/19-20 Soi Sarasin, ph 250 0103), *Blue-Jazz* (25 Sukhumvit Road, ph 258 7747) and *Saxaphone* (near Victory Monument, ph 246 5472).

Rock concerts are held at *Capital City*, on Ratchadapisek Road. *Rocky Pub* (119/62-63 Phaya Thai Road, near *McKenna Theatre)*, plays loud and heavy rock.

Cultural Events and Venues

Bangkok night life doesn't just revolve around bars and clubs. Other events are held irregularly and the daily newspapers are best consulted. The *Bangkok Symphony Orchestra* performs occasionally. Some embassies also have cultural events.

There are a few theatre groups in the capital including: *Bangkok Theatre Playhouse* (2884/2 New Petchburi Road, ph 319 7641), *Bangkok Community Theatre* (ph 319 7641) and the *Thai Cultural Centre* (Main Hall, Ratchadapisek Road, ph 247 0013).

Art galleries are scattered throughout Bangkok and regular exhibitions also occur in the embassies. The papers are the best source of information on what is happening. Contact the following galleries for more details; *Art Forum* (ph 271 4086), *Aua* (ph 252 8170), *Ideal Art Centre* (ph 253 1545), *National Museum* (ph 224 1333), *Saeng Arun Art Centre* (ph 237 0080), and *Studio Xang* (ph 241 1531).

Queen Sirikit National Convention Centre

Located at 60 New Ratchadapisek Road, ph 229 3000, fax 229 4253, the centre provides a variety of entertainment events from conventions and concerts to displays. The head office of *Bangkok Airways* is also located here. The restaurants, especially *Lakeside Restaurant and Terrace* overlooking the lake, are also popular.

Cinema

There are both English-speaking and Thai movie theatres in Bangkok. Most movies start around midday with other sessions at 2pm, 5pm, 7.17pm and 9.15pm. An additional session at 10am is held on weekends and holidays. Admission ranges from B30 to B70 depending on the movie, venue and air conditioning. The *Bangkae 10* at *Future Park*, ph 454 8708, is the ultimate cinema experience with ten theatres from which to choose.

Some embassies and educational institutes also show movies. *Alliance Francaise* (29 Sathorn Tai Road, ph 213 2122) for example, has regular movies. Other film venues include: *Goethe Institute* (18/1 Soi Attakamprasit Road, ph 286 9002) and the *Japanese Cultural Centre* (10th Fl, Sermit Tower, Sukhumvit, Soi 21, ph 260 8560).

If all else fails, stay in your hotel and watch any number of satellite TV channels.

Dance Clubs

Silom Road, Soi 4 is Bangkok's latest dance favourite with the smartest clubs and bars. Some you can try are: *Rome Club, Deeper, Sphinx, Paparazzi, Ugly Club, Deep, Milk Bar* and *Telephone.*

Massage

Thai massage is an old, respected art, but all the massage parlours, of which there are hundreds, are not necessarily masters of the art. Traditional massage is an ancient therapy based on yoga, reflexology and acupressure. It is not soft and gentle so be prepared for a little discomfort as your body is contorted into positions you never thought possible. Rest assured, you will feel better for it after. Allow up to two to three hours to appreciate the full effects.

If you would like to experience a true massage, or health massage, it is best to check with your hotel information counter for suggestions. However, the following is a good guide: *Bavorn Number One* (ph 253 7791), *Bodie Care* (ph 238 4680), *Wat Pho* (Chetuphon Road; this is the spiritual home of the ancient therapy where you can be massaged or learn the art).

Shopping

Few cities equal Bangkok as a shopper's paradise. Exclusive boutiques cater to those for whom money is no object and the many rip-off stalls in the markets cater to those who aspire to feeling that money is no object.

Indra Regent-Pratunam Markets is a favourite haunt for bargain hunters. There are many optical shops in the hotel's arcade, and rip-off merchandise in the surrounding shops and stalls.

Siam Square. This is another sprawling shopping area selling virtually anything. There are several movie theatres and fast food restaurants. Opposite *Siam Square* is *Discovery Center* and *Siam Centre* (one of Bangkok's trendiest complexes selling local and foreign designer labels) and *Mah Boon Krong Centre* (excellent boutique shopping and *Tokyu* Department Store).

Seacon Square, Srinakarin Road, next to the *Seri Centre,* is the world's fifth largest shopping centre. It has four main traders; *Robinson Department Store, Yoyo Funplay Land, DK Bookstore* (owned by the Bangkok icon, Khun Suk) and *Lotus Supercentre.*

Silom Village at 286 Silom Road, ph 234 4448, is styled along the lines of Old Bangkok and has shops, restaurants and *Ruen Thep* traditional classical dance in the evening. Antiques and handicrafts shops are situated in a garden village. While this is a bit touristy it's good if you are only in Bangkok a short time and want to sample Thai culture.

Robinsons and *Central Department Stores* (now under the one ownership) are Thailand's big department stores. Other leading retailers, especially Japanese-owned (*Sogo, Zen, Isetan* and *Tokyu*), have stores in Bangkok. Prices here are fixed, so no bartering, but they all facilitate shopping by accepting credit cards. *Zen* and *Isetan,* in the *World Trade Centre* are well located. *Isetan* has *Jim Thompson* and *Oriental* shops in the store.

Gaysorn Plaza, opposite the *Erewan Shrine,* has leading designer boutiques amongst fashionable restaurants including *Planet Hollywood.*

Other shops and centres worth visiting include: *Narayana Phand,* 127 Ratchamri Road (handicrafts) and *Tower Records* (music at the top of *Siam Centre*),

Sightseeing

Bangkok is home to many *wats*, or temples; over 400 in fact. No visit to Bangkok is complete without visiting at least a few. It is possible to see much of Bangkok using this guide book and public transport. An alternative is to go on an organised tour and let someone else find the sights in a crowded city. The former is adventurous fun but the latter, easier.

Chao Phraya River

The river is one of Asia's best known and a feature of Bangkok. Sitting along the banks can be lots of fun as ferries, rice barges and longtail boats constantly move along and across the river. Travelling on the river is just as eventful. The *Chao Phaya Express Ferry* is a good orientation. *Wat Arun* gives a spectacular elevated view. The following hotels are pleasant havens for a *Singha* or two; the Royal Orchid Sheraton, Oriental, Shangri-la, Menam, Sofitel and Royal River.

Chinatown

Chinatown is located just to the south-east of what was the

former city centre, around the Grand Palace. Here you can see Goldshop Street and a variety of other stores, many of which are down narrow crowded lanes.

Around Democracy Monument

Democracy Monument

At the intersection of Rajdamnern Klang Avenue and Dinsor is the monument erected in 1932 to commemorate the nation's first constitution. It was also the centre of the military killings in the May 1992 democratic protests.

Wat Saket

The Golden Mount, as it is commonly know, provides a good elevated view of Bangkok. It is located near Bamrung Muang Road and is open daily. There is a small entry fee to the most elevated point of the temple.

Dusit Zoo

The zoo is a pleasant retreat for humans but maybe not so for the animals caged in the tropical heat. It is located on Rama V Road and here you will find many Asian animals such as elephants, gibbons, monkeys, rhinos, orang utans, bears, tigers, birds and reptiles. The open grasslands and peaceful setting make it a pleasant recreation spot, especially if you are travelling with children. It is open daily 8am-6pm with a B10 entry fee.

Vimanmek Mansion (Celestial Residence)

This 81 room mansion was built in 1901 as King Rama V's residence. It has been renovated and opened as a museum. A little piece of trivia; this is the world's largest golden teak building! The mansions are located off U-Thong Road, near the Dusit Zoo. It is open daily 9.30am-3.15pm with a B50 entry fee which includes a guided tour (ph 281 4715). It is sometimes spelt with a "w" and not a "v". There is a series of museums containing royal gifts, photos, paintings and royal carriages. There are several daily displays of dancing.

Around Siam Square

Erewan Shrine

Tucked in between the *Grand Hyatt Erewan Hotel* and *Sogo Department Store*, at the intersection of Ratchadamn and Ploenchit Roads, is one of Bangkok's more interesting tourist attractions. While the original *Erewan Hotel* was under construction on the site in 1956, a series of unexplained accidents plagued the work. The story goes that the spirits who lived in trees on the site had been deprived of a home when they were cut down. The owner erected a temple for them and there were no further problems. The small Brahmin shrine, San Phra Prom is the centre of attraction for many Buddhist worshippers and tourists. Resident female classical dancers are on hand to dance, for a fee. Hiring the dancers and buying small teak elephants is a way of thanking the spirits. 'Erewan' refers to a royal three-headed elephant, ridden by Indra in Hindu beliefs; that's why there are so many wooden elephants here.

Jim Thompson's House

New York Architect, Jim Thompson came to Thailand at the end of WWII and became interested in the silk industry. He was instrumental in Thai silk becoming world renowned. On 26.3.68 he went for an afternoon stroll while holidaying in Malaysia's Cameron Highlands, and never returned. His antique-filled house situated at 6 Soi Kasemsan 2, just off Rama 1 Road opposite the National Stadium (ph 215 0122), is open Mon-Sat, 9am-4.30pm. There is a rather steep entry fee of B100, but all proceeds go to charity. There are actually six houses, which are all authentic and have been dismantled and brought from various parts of the country. The garden setting is very relaxing and there is a shop selling silk products. Jim Thompson products can also be found in stores throughout the city.

Around the River

Floating Market

The old market on the Thonburi side of the Chao Phraya still operates but is mostly visited by tourists. There won't be any bargains in the shops, but the trip is worth it to see the klongs.

You can go on an organised tour, or hire your own longtail boat for an hour or so for about half the cost.

Wat Pho (Wat Chetuphon or the Temple of the Reclining Buddha)

Founded in the 16th century, it is the oldest and largest temple with the greatest number of pagodas (950) in the city. It is principally known for its 46m x 15m high, reclining Buddha. The room housing the Buddha is barely bigger than it and therefore it is difficult to get an overall perspective. Forget about photos unless you have a super wide angle lens. Essentially, all that can be seen are the soles of the feet which are covered with mother-of-pearl, illustrating the marks and qualities of Buddha. It is open daily 8am-5pm and costs B10 to enter. Masseurs are available for traditional massages, at a cost.

Grand Palace and Wat Phra Kaeo

If you see anything in Bangkok, you must see the Royal Palace and the Emerald Buddha housed in *Wat Phra Kaeo*. While only 75 cm tall, it is the most sacred Buddhist image in Thailand and was carved from a single block of jade in the 15th century. The statue originates from a small temple of the same name in Chiang Rai. It is placed under a huge parasol, and has three different sets of clothes; gold for the hot season, diamonds for the cold season and blue spangles for the rainy season. Surrounding the royal chapel is the cloister, with galleries adorned with frescoes illustrating the Ramakien and the exploits of Hanuman, the monkey-god. These date from the late 18th century and are constantly restored.

The Grand Palace is a walled city founded in 1782 by King Rama 1. It was not only the King's home but also the seat of government. *Chakri Maha Prasad* is the main building, and is a mixture of Thai and Victorian architecture. The throne room is located here but it is not open to the public. Most visitors will relate to the palace as the setting for the book, *Anna and the King of Siam* and the movie, *The King and I* (a movie still banned in Thailand). Most Thais agree that much of the story was fictional.

There is a model of the famous Cambodia temple, *Angkor Wat*, in the Grand Palace. Many of the bonsai plants in the grounds are believed to be up to 400 years old. The palace is open daily 8.30am-3.30pm and entry is B100.

National Museum

The museum on Na Prathet Road is the largest of its kind in South-East Asia and houses Thailand's artistic treasures. It is open Wed-Sun 9am-4pm, and the entry fee is B30. Volunteers conduct tours in a variety of languages.

Royal Barge Museum

Located on Klong Bangkok Noi, this building is a little hard to find and is best accessed by boat. The barges are used in royal ceremonies on the Chao Phraya River. The museum is open 9am-4pm and entry is B10.

During Kathin, the ceremony at the end of the Buddhist retreat, the King, accompanied by 51 boats proceeds to *Wat Arun* to present the monks with new saffron robes.

Wat Arun

The Temple of Dawn, as it is commonly known, is located beside the Chao Phraya River opposite *Wat Po* and Chinatown. The temple looks spectacular at anytime of the day but particularly in the early evening when the lights are turned on. The millions of tiny pieces of porcelain that adorn the *prangs* radiate an energetic light. The central *prang* is the height of a 20 storey building (104m) and the view of the city and river is one of the city's best. The climb to the top is steep however and the steps small. Be careful! It opens daily with a small admission fee.

Other parts of the City

Pasteur Institute's Snake Farm

Some of the world's most venomous snakes are kept at the farm on Rama IV Road for venom extraction to make snake serum. It is open daily 8.30am-4pm and entry is B80. There are daily snakes shows when snake venom is 'milked'.

Wat Benchamabophit

Otherwise known as the Marble Temple, this *wat* is one of the best examples of modern Thai *wat* architecture. It was the last major Buddhist temple to be built in the city and now houses a replica of the beautiful Phra Phutthachinarat Buddha, a famous image from Phitsanulok. Behind the back court there are 53

Buddha images representing major Asian styles.

While many are copies, they provide a reference for Asian Buddhist sculpture. It is located on Rama V Road and is open daily with an entry fee of B10.

Wat Traimit

The world's largest solid gold Buddha is housed in this *wat* located near Hualamphong Station. It is about 800 years old, 3m high and weighs 5.5 tonnes. For centuries, the gold was hidden behind a layer of stucco. In 1957, the gold was exposed when the statue fell and cracked while being transported. The *wat* is open daily 9am-5pm and entry is B10.

Weekend Market

Located on 13ha of land at Chatuchak Park on Phahonyothin Road, the 5500 stall markets are very popular for almost everything and bartering is the name of the game. These markets were once located at Sanam Luang. They are open 8.30am-4pm. Other popular markets include those at Bangrak, Thewes Market (plants), Pratunam, Patpong Night Markets and Phak Klong Talat (located near the Reclining Buddha and is especially good for flowers). There was once a big illegal trade in endangered animals here but this appears to have moved elsewhere or gone underground.

Outlying Attractions

Just 32km or one hour west of Bangkok (depending on the traffic) on the Nakhon Pathom Road is a riverside tropical park and country club. If you only have a short time in Thailand and want to have a theme park idea of Thai culture, the *Rose Garden* has it all (Thai wedding ceremony, Buddhist ordination and elephants). There are cultural performances at 2.15pm and 3.15pm daily. Accommodation is available with full resort facilities such as restaurants, bar, 18-hole golf, tennis, shops and pool. There are 100 rooms from B1800. ph (034) 311 171, fax (02) 253 2625. Nearby, the *Samphran Elephant Ground and Zoo* has an entertaining collection of animals.

Crocodile Farm, 30km south of Bangkok, has 30,000 reptiles, the largest collection of its type in the world. Almost next door in Muang Boran is the *Ancient City* (ph 221 4495) which has

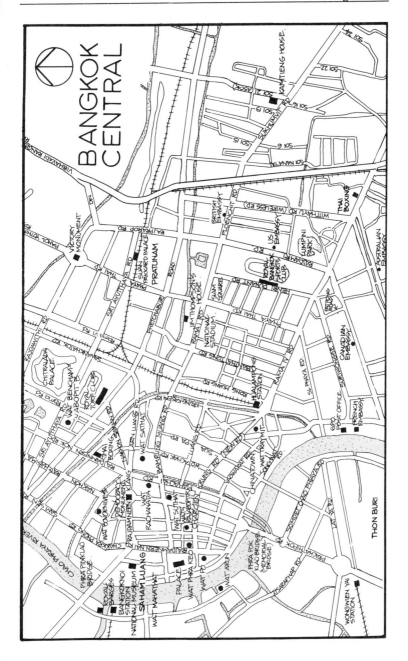

scaled-down reproductions of the kingdom's famous temples.

Safari World is located to the north of the city on Raminthra Road. Here it is possible to drive through a wildlife park and see tigers, lions and other animals. There is also a bird park attached, ph 395 1477.

Nakhon Pathom

Phra Pathom Chedi, at 130m high, is the world's tallest Buddhist image. The yellowish-brown, bell-shaped, chedi dominates the skyline in the city, some 60km to the west of Bangkok. The city is supposedly the oldest in Thailand. Buses and trains from the south and Bangkok to the east serve the town. *Buddha Monthon*, on the way to Nakhon Pathom, celebrates the 2500th anniversary of Buddhism.

The telephone area code is 034. Places to stay include: *Nakhon Inn* (ph 251 152, from B80), *Suthahip* (ph 242 242, from B110) and *Whale* (ph 251 020, from B320). A trip to the town can be linked with a visit to Damnoen Saduak floating market or as a stop-off while travelling south. Most visitors pass through the town and don't stop over.

Damnoen Saduak

Located in Ratchaburi Province, 80km south-west of Bangkok, is the 'new' Bangkok floating markets, or the one on most tour operators' itineraries. The photographs of these floating markets have probably sold more holidays to Thailand than any other image. Like most Asian markets, the action happens between 6.30 and 8am. After that, most activity is purely for tourists. I am sure when I was last there, villagers were circling the markets in their boats just for tourists to photograph them. It does make good photography though early in the morning if you can get there before the tour buses.

Bang Pa-In

About 50km north of Bangkok (40km south of Ayutthaya), Bang Pa-In is the site of the summer or country residence of the Kings of Ayutthaya. It was destroyed by the Burmese, and the present buildings date from the late 19th century. There is a lake with an island on which stands the **Aisawan Thi Paya**, the best known pavilion in the complex and a fine example of Thai architecture. It contains a statue of King Chulalongkorn, once a regular visitor. The **Royal Palace** consists of five buildings, built in Thai, Chinese, Italian and Victorian styles. In the centre of the grounds is the **Wehat Chamrun** (Chinese Pavilion) which was presented to the king by the Thai-Chinese community in gratitude for their welcome into the country. They are all located in a park which is open Mon-Sat, 8.30am-4pm. It costs B50 to enter. Bang Pa-In and Ayutthaya are normally visited on the same tour. Buses and trains going to and from Ayutthaya service Bang Pa-In.

Close to Bang Pa-In (in Tambon Bung Yai) is the *Bang Sai Folk Arts and Craft Centre* with displays of traditional handicrafts. Established in 1976, it aims to teach farmers traditional artisan skills to supplement their agricultural income. Products such as baskets, artificial flowers, silk, cotton, furniture and clothes are made and sold here.

Ayutthaya

At its peak, Ayutthaya had 100 *wats* and thousands of Buddhists images. It was the Thai capital for more than 400 years until 1767 when the city was sacked and detroyed by the Burmese. In its heyday, it was one of Asia's most famous cities with maybe as many as one million inhabitants. It was situated on an island guarded by a moat formed by three rivers. There were three palaces; Grand Palace, Chankasem Palace (Front Palace) and Wang Lang (Rear Palace). In addition, there were many monasteries. It's wealth attracted merchants from Europe and Asia. Today it is recognised as a UNESCO World Heritage Site.

The city is 80km from the capital and travelling time varies according to the traffic. The train offers an enjoyable journey through the green patchwork rice paddies of the Chao Phraya floodplain. The *Oriental Queen* (ph 236 0400) river cruiser and the *Chao Phraya Express Boat Company* (ph 222 5330) have cruises to the city. The former charges B1,100 (includes daily cruise, lunch and tour) and the latter from B180 (operates on Sun only). Many cruises stop on the way back at *Wat Phai Lom* to look at a bird sanctuary for the rare open-billed stork.

The telephone area code is 035.

How to Get There

By Rail
Every Sat and Sun the State Railway Authority of Thailand, in conjunction with *River Sun Cruise*, offers a day trip to Ayutthaya and Bang Pa-In. The train leaves at 6.30am and you return to Bangkok with a cruise down the Chao Phraya River. Reservations can be made on ph 225 6964 ext 4217, or ring *River Sun Cruises*, ph 237 0077.

Daily train services leave Bangkok every hour 5.20am to 11.25pm, and the trip takes 1 hour 30 minutes.

By Bus
Direct AC buses leave Bangkok's Northern terminal hourly 6am-6pm and cost B40.

Tourist Information
The TAT Office is located at Si Sanphet Road, Ayutthaya, ph 246 076, fax 246 078.

Accommodation
Ayutthaya Grand, 55/5 Rochana Road, ph 244 483, fax 244 492. 122 AC rooms, restaurant, bar and pool. From B700.
B.J. Guest House, 16/7 Naresuan Road, ph 251 512. 8 rooms with fans from B40.
Cathay, 36/5 U Thong Road, ph 251 662. 26 rooms with fans. From B90.

Sightseeing
Attractions focus on the ancient ruins of the former capital, most of which were destroyed by the Burmese who plundered the city in 1767. Not all the temples have been covered in this section, and others include: *Wat Phraram, Wat Lokkayasutha, Wat Phutthaisawan, Wat Na Phramen, Wat Kudidao* to name a few.

The temples are scattered over a large area and some form of transport is needed. Tuk tuks can be hired on a daily basis for about B250 to B300.

Chankasem Palace

The palace was built on the banks of the Pasak River as a residence for the King's son. The Phlapphla Chaturamuk building is now a National Museum open Wed-Sun, 9am-4pm.

Chao Sam Phraya National Museum

The museum is located on Rochana Road, opposite the city wall, and houses antique bronze images, carved panels and relics. It is open Wed-Sun, 9am-4pm and admission is B10. Also on Rachana Road, is the *Ayutthaya Historical Study Centre* (ph 244 769), a national research institute devoted to the study of Ayutthaya. It looks after the museum and a library. It is open Wed-Sun, 9am-4pm and admission is B100.

Grand Palace

Currently called the Ancient Palace, there are several important buildings in the compound, including halls to witness royal barge processions, coronation halls and residential buildings. Some structures date to 1350.

Wang Lang

This was once a garden retreat for the King and only contained one building; a residence.

Wat Phra Si Sanphet

It is located in the Grand Palace and was a residence before it became a *wat*. Construction began in 1384 but several additions have been made since. The 16m bronze Buddha statue is dominant.

Wat Phra Mahathat

This is the biggest of Ayutthaya's temples and is located in front of the Grand Palace. It was built in 1384 with many sections being added over the centuries. Entry fee is B20.

Wat Ratchaburana

Located opposite Wat Phra Mahathat, the Khmer-style *prang* is a burial place for two of the then King's brothers.

Tours

The *Siam Society* conducts historical and archaeological tours in and around Bangkok and Thailand for their members. Contact them on ph 260 2830, fax 258 3491.

The *Wildlife Fund of Thailand* conducts nature and culture-based tours throughout Bangkok, the country and the region. Call them on ph 521 3435 for more details.

Commercial tours of Bangkok operated by professional tour companies are available from tour desks at all large hotels. They are sold as half day or full day tours, and will visit a combination of the following destinations: *Grand Palace, Jim Thompson's House, Wat Benchamabophit, Wat Arun, Floating Markets, Crocodile Farm* as well as more distant destinations like *Rose Gardens, Ayutthaya* and *Damnern Saduak Floating Markets*.

Sport and Recreation

Popular sports in the city include badminton, 10-pin bowling, soccer, ice-skating, rugby, snooker, squash, tennis and kick boxing. The *Hash House Harriers* (ph 252 8997) and *Hash House Bikers* (ph 252 3677) have regular outings followed by much 'on, on-ing'. Runs are generally advertised in the sporting columns of the papers.

Golf

There are many clubs and courses within close proximity to Bangkok. They generally open from 6am to dusk. The following clubs are recommended: *Asian Institute of Technology* (ph 516 0110 ext 5267), *Royal Bangkok Sports Club* (ph 251 0181), *Rose Garden* (ph (034) 322 771) and *Kan Tarat* (ph 534 3840, located at Don Muang International Airport).

Horse Racing

Although not unique to Thailand, Thai punters have unequalled passion for racing. On course betting starts at B50 but the sky's the limit. There are two race courses in Bangkok offering events on alternate Sundays. The *Royal Turf Club* (ph 280 0020) and *The Royal Bangkok Sports Club* (ph 251 0181) are the venues.

Ice Skating
World Ice Skating Centre (ph 255 9500) is located in the *Trade World Centre* and you can ice skate while others swelter outside in the tropical heat. There are other rinks at *Mall 4*, Ramkamhaeng (ph 318 1001) and *Mall 5*, Thonburi (ph 477 9018).

Sports Clubs
Most large hotels have sporting facilities and usually non-hotel residents can use these facilities for a small charge. There are several sporting clubs in Bangkok and most operate on annual memberships for long term visitors and locals but they may accept casual visitors. Facilities at such clubs usually include a pool, tennis, squash, gyms, badminton, spas and saunas. Most operate regular fitness and aerobics classes. Contact the following for more details: *71 Sport Club* (ph 391 6773), *Royal Bangkok Sports Club* (ph 251 0181) and the *British Club* (234 0247).

Thai Boxing
There are two main boxing stadiums in Bangkok, Rajdamnoen (ph 281 4205) and Lumpini (251 4303) where there are fights on Tues, Fri and Sat. Thais love watching Thai and normal boxing, just watch them crowd around TVs when there is a fight in progress.

Bridge over the River Kwai

Kanchanaburi - River Kwai

The town is renowned for the famous bridge over the River Kwai (pronounced *kwa,* in Thai; ie without emphasising the 'i'). The black iron bridge, originally from Java, featured in the movie *Bridge Over the River Kwai* and in Boulle's book of the same name. The movie was actually filmed in Sri Lanka and not Thailand. The rail bridge was part of the Death Railway built by thousands of prisoners of war and impressed Asian labourers during WWII. One of the highlights is the River Kwai Bridge Week in late November to early December. The week's festival includes steam train rides, and a nightly sound and light show that re-enacts the WWII Allied bombing of the bridge.

The province is noted for its rugged scenery and mountains that border Myanmar. These mountains are often covered in mist and the valleys are dissected by rapidly flowing streams. The natural scenery is some of the more spectacular in the Kingdom. This water has been dammed for hydro-electricity in several locations. The province is popular with international tourists and locals because of its natural environment, history and close proximity to Bangkok. The telephone area code is 034.

How to Get There

By Road

The city is 130km, or three hours bus journey, from Bangkok. Regular and AC buses leave the Southern Bus Terminal frequently. From Kanchanaburi regular buses leave for Bangkok every ten minutes from 3.30am to 6.30pm. AC buses leave every 15 minutes between 4am and 7pm. Buses also go to the floating markets at Damnoen Saduak, Cha Am and Hua Hin. If you are travelling to, or coming from the north, and don't want to go back to Bangkok you can head to Supanburi and Ayutthaya to connect with the train or bus.

By Rail
Trains leave Bangkok Noi station in Thonburi; make sure you don't go to the main train station. Trains to Kanchanaburi leave Thonburi at 8am and 1.40pm, arriving 2½ hours later. They continue up the Death Railway arriving at Nam Tok Station terminus at 12.20pm and 6.30pm. The return trip leaves at 6.05am and 12.35pm, crossing the River Kwai Bridge at 8am and 2.25pm; and reaching Bangkok Noi at 10.50am and 5.10pm. The whole trip costs B41 in 3rd class, one way. It costs B2 to just ride across the bridge and into Kanchanaburi. On Saturday, Sunday and public holidays, a special train goes from Thonburi to Nam Tok at 6.35am, arriving at 11.40am. It returns at 2.40pm, arriving Thonburi at 7.35pm. The return fare is B75.

Tourist Information
The TAT Office is in Saeng Chuto Road, Amphoe Muang, Kanchanaburi, ph/fax 511 200.

Accommodation
Accommodation is either found in hotels and guest houses around the city or in lodges along the River Kwai. Some of the river lodges are out of town and only accessible by boat. They certainly are pleasant but if access is important it may be best to stay in town. There are a few riverside lodges in town offering visitors both the city and the river. There are four national parks in the province, all with accommodation. Bookings to the Bangkok office, ph 579 5025, are recommended.

Kwai Noi Island Resort, 103 Moo 4 Tambon Wang Yen, ph (01) 313 6420. From B600.

Pavilion Rimkwai Resort, Kanchanaburi to Ladya Road, ph 255 3296, fax 286 2681. From B2,700.

River Kwai Jungle House (Ban Rim Kwai). In Sai Yok district north, on the River Kwai, north of Kanchanaburi. The entrance is located opposite Wang-Pho viaduct, ph 561 052. 80 rooms from B680/person, including meals and tours.

Sam's Place, Song Kwai Road (besides the river), ph 513 971. AC or fan, rafts, bathrooms, restaurant, IDD in lobby, and tours available. From B150 to B250. Don't plan on an early night here as the next door entertainment will keep you awake.

Local Transport

Kanchanaburi is an elongated town along the river and is too big to walk around comfortably. The TAT Office has a good leaflet with the latest timetables and best way to access nearby tourist destinations on public transport. Some guest houses hire out bikes, while buses and *songthaews* go up and down the highway. Expect to pay about B10 to most places. There are also rickshaws in town and if you arrive by bus or train they will eagerly take you to your accommodation for about B20. The real reward for rickshaw drivers is in the 'spotter's fee' paid by the guest house owner for your patronage. Longtail boats also operate on the river. It is best to find others interested in destinations near yours as the rate is the same for one or ten. Expect to pay about B1,200/boat to see the Lawa Caves and Sai Yok Yai Waterfall. Trains can be used locally to access destinations along the Kwai River (*see How To Get There, for the train service*). For example, Prasat Muang Singh Historic Park is best served by train. A local train to Nam Tok leaves Kanchanaburi Station each day at 6am, arriving at 8.25am.

Eating Out and Entertainment

The best eating places in town are the many stalls or floating restaurants along the river. These are found along Song Kwai Road in the vicinity of *Sam's Guest House.* Tourist-oriented, floating restaurants are located below the bridge and best avoided during the day when the tour buses pull in. Beyond eating, there is really only karaoke and the Thai cinema (near the bus terminal). Kanchanaburi is a good place to catch up on sleep, the exception is during River Kwai Bridge Week.

Shopping

Kanchanaburi is not noted as a shopping destination unless you are in the market for a River Kwai T-shirt or postcard. Blue sapphires mined in nearby Bo Phloi are available. Read the section on *Gemstones* under *Shopping* in the *Travel Information* chapter about warnings on buying 'gemstones'.

Sightseeing

Kanchanaburi was the main base for constructing the Death
Railway during World War II. To many, it is a sobering
reminder of the horrors of war. Some 16,000 Allied prisoners of
war died laying the train line that linked Rangoon (capital of
present day Myanmar and now called Yangon) with the existing
rail track at Ban Pong, west of Bangkok. Many Asians, also
forced to work on this track, suffered the same fate. Other
attractions near the town are historical and natural features in
the national parks.

Bo Phloi

This gem town (sapphires and onyx) is located 48km from
Kanchanaburi.

Bridge Over the River Kwai

In 1942, the Japanese, who then occupied Thailand, decided to
develop a more secure route between Rangoon and Thailand.
The rail line between Thanbyuzayat in Burma and Ban Pong
began in 1942 and the link was made on 25.10.43 at Neike just
below the Three Pagodas Pass. The strategic bridge across the
river came from Java and was reassembled on site. The bridge
was a target for frequent Allied bombing during 1945 and it was
rebuilt after the war.

It is possible to walk across the bridge except when the train
crosses. Watch out for motorcyclists who also use the bridge. If
you are there in the afternoon, you can get on the train on the
western side of the river and ride it to the station or into
Kanchanaburi for B2. There are a few restaurants, souvenir
shops and an old train near the River Kwai Station.

Death Railway

The railway line from Kanchanaburi to Nam Tok is one of the
most infamous in Asia, if not the world.

Kanchanaburi War Cemetery

The immaculately kept grounds of the cemetery are located on
the northern end of the main road, opposite the train station.
There are two other Allied graveyards at Chungkai and

Thanbyuzayat, but this is the main one and contains the remains of about 7000 prisoners of war, including 1362 Australians, who died laying the rail tracks. It has been estimated that one in five died working on the line. Despite the traffic noise there is a sombre tranquillity in the grounds. The memorial plaques make interesting reading, none more relevant than the one which says, *"someday, I may understand"*. Chon-Kai War Cemetery, is 2km away and contains the remains of 1750 soldiers.

Lawa Caves
The limestone caves are 75km from town and accessible by boat. Daowadung Caves are also worth exploring.

Muang Singha Historic Park
Best to go by train if using public transport. Trains leave Kanchanaburi for Thakilen Station at 6am and 10.30am. Trains from Nam Tok depart Thakilen Station at 7.06am, 1.34pm and 4.31pm and take one hour to reach Kanchanaburi.

River Kwai Rafting
Day or overnight rafting is becoming increasingly popular on both the River Kwai and River Kwai Noi. This is best done as a group activity as a whole raft is hired whether it is one person or 15. Daily charges range up to B4500. Travel agents or TAT in either Bangkok or Kanchanaburi can provide further details.

Sai Yok Yai Waterfall
The falls are 60km north of Kanchanaburi. They are located near the road and 2km north of Nam Tok Station, making them very accessible. Buses leave Kanchanaburi regularly between 6.45am and 6pm.

The JEATH War Museum
JEATH stands for Japan, England, America, Australia, Thailand and Holland; the main, but not only, nations involved in the conflict in Kanchanaburi. The museum has recreated the camp as it was during the war and contains many authentic pieces donated by survivors. It is located in the grounds of *Wat Chai Chumphon* and is open from 8.30am to 6pm. Entry is B20.

Sangklaburi - Three Pagodas Pass

The border town of Three Pagodas Pass (the town on the Myanmar side is called Payathonzu), 340km from Bangkok (225km from Kanchanaburi), has always been a trading centre. Myanmar, previously off limits to all but passengers arriving by air in Yangon, has relaxed these immigration restrictions. The arrangement for foreigners wanting to enter is the same for Mai Sai in northern Thailand. Basically, you surrender your passport to the Thai officials and hand over B130 to the Myanmar officials.

Not surprisingly, there are three white pagodas near the border. The town has always been strategically important. During the Ayutthaya Period (1350 to 1767), Burmese soldiers invaded Thailand via this route. It was a station on the Death Railway during WWII, and more recently, Mon and Karen minority groups in Myanmar have attacked the SLORC military forces now controlling Myanmar. Trading has temporarily replaced fighting and inside Myanmar there is a market town selling traditional handicrafts and fabrics. It depends on what interests you, but you could spend an hour in Payathonzu or all day. If you have made the effort, and are staying in the area, spend the day as the Myanmar people are very friendly, love talking to foreigners and enjoy having their photos taken.

The town is accessible from Bangkok in a gruelling day's travel. The first bus leaves for Kanchanaburi at 5.30am. This goes via Thong Pah Phum and connects with a bus to Sangklaburi and then a *songthaew* ride to the border. You need to be back in Sangklaburi by 3.30pm to start the journey home. More easily, you should set off from Kanchanaburi where regular buses leave from 6.45am to 1.50pm but take five hours. Mini buses do it in just over three hours between 7.30am to 4.30pm. From Sangklaburi, the mini buses leave between 6.30am and 3.30pm. The fare for both is B100. Local buses are more interesting as you see more, however, they are slower. A good idea is to go by local bus one way and mini bus on the return leg.

If you want to stay in the district there is accommodation at Thong Pah Phum and Sangklaburi. Six kilometres from Thong Pah Phum, and 2km from the road is a bungalow resort built in the middle of the forest. The rooms have AC and bathrooms and cost from B400. It is probably best to go all the way to Sangklaburi where there is some choice. Try *P Guest House* (ph 595 061) or *Burmese Inn* (from B45) or *Sreedang Hotel*, near Sangklaburi market, ph 595 039 (AC or fan rooms with attached bathroom, from B160 to B800). The hotel is central, clean and has a good restaurant (some dishes are written in wonderful bastardised English) but must have the thinnest walls of all the hotels in Thailand; ask for a room well away from others. *Three Pagodas Resort* is on the right hand side of the main road into the small town, ph 595 316. The 60 bungalow resort is the only place in town but is very overpriced at B1000 considering the limited range of facilities. It would be far better to stay in Sangklaburi and travel 30 minutes in a *songthaew* than stay here.

Other attractions around Sangklaburi include *Khao Laem Dam* and elephant trekking. The road from Thong Pha Phum traverses the lake for 70km providing a highly picturesque journey. Houseboat accommodation is available on the lake.

Erewan National Park

The seven-tiered Erewan falls are one of the most photographed falls in the country and deservedly so. They are the main feature in the park but the limestone caves (*Phrathat Caves*) and bamboo forests also attract nature lovers. Bungalow accommodation is available in the park and should be booked in Bangkok, ph (02) 579 0529.

Buses leave Kanchanaburi for the falls every hour between 8am and 4pm, and the journey takes two hours. The last bus back leaves at 4pm and is usually packed at the weekends.

Cha Am and Hua Hin

Cha Am and Hua Hin are two adjoining seaside resorts in Prachuap Khiri Khan Province, about 178 and 203km respectively, south of Bangkok. The resorts stretch down the Gulf of Thailand with Myanmar to the west, at the narrowest point, only 12km away. They are tranquil retreats as opposed to the brashness of Pattaya on the other side of the Gulf of Thailand. If you want a reasonably quiet seaside escape from Bangkok, this is probably the best, and the closest to the capital. After travelling through Thailand, Hua Hin makes a pleasant 'holiday' before returning home. While the two destinations are only 25km apart, development is slowly connecting both.

The phone code is 032.

How to Get There

By Air
Bangkok Airways (in Bangkok ph 229 3456, in Hua Hin ph 512 083) has a daily Dash 8 service from Bangkok in the morning. The flight only takes 40 minutes, and the airport is ten minutes from Hua Hin. There is a limousine service to town, although major hotels have pick-up services.

By Rail
The main north-south train line from Bangkok to Singapore goes through both Hua Hin and Cha Am. Most international trains from the south arrive at Hua Hin early in the morning. Travelling time from Bangkok is just over three hours, depending on the type of train.

By Road
Regular (ph 02-434 5557) and AC (ph 02-435 5032) buses leave

the Southern Bus Terminal for Cha Am, Hua Hin and Prachuap Khiri Khan. Regular services go in both directions. Trips to Bangkok take about three hours.

By Boat
Thai Intertransport (ph 02 291 9617) operates a passenger hydrofoil service between Bangkok, Hua Hin and Pattaya.

Tourist Information
The TAT Office is at 500/51 Phetkasem Road, Cha Am. ph 471 005, fax 471 502.

Accommodation
The following information, particularly the prices, should be used as a guide only. Many places offer discounts in the off season as well as applying a high season surcharge. Most are best booked as a package. The telephone area code is 032.

All Nations Guest House, 10/1 Daechanuchit Road, Hua Hin, ph 512 747. 12 rooms, satellite TV, videos and bar. From B120.

Cha Am Cabana Resort, 186 Klongtien Road, Cha Am, ph 471 861. From B800.

Cha Am Inn, 244 Naratip Road, Cha Am, ph 471 536. From B200.

Fulay Guest House, 110/1 Naresdamri Road, Hua Hin, ph 513 670. 9 AC rooms, TV, mini-bar and sea views. From B750.

Jed Pee Nong, 17 Damnoenkasem Road, Hua Hin, ph 512 381. Rooms with AC or fans, restaurant and pool. From B400.

Melia Hua Hin, 33/3 Naresdamri Road, Hua Hin, ph 512 879, fax 511 135. 297 AC rooms, satellite TV, inhouse movies, personal safe, restaurants (Chinese and Mediterranean), pool, tennis, squash and gym. From B3000.

Royal Garden Resort, 107/1 Phetkasem Beach Road, Hua Hin, ph 511 881, fax 512 422. 221 AC rooms, IDD, satellite TV, restaurants, water sports, pool, tennis and disco. From B2800.

Royal Garden Village, 43/1 Phetkasem Beach Road, Hua Hin, ph 520 250, fax 520 259. 162 AC, Thai-style villas, extensive gardens, IDD, satellite TV, restaurants, water sports, pool, and tennis. From B3700.

Sofitel Central, Damnoenkasem Road, Hua Hin, ph 512 021, fax 511 014. 216 AC rooms, IDD, satellite TV, mini-bar, restaurants, tennis, watersports, pools, nightclub, shops and extensive gardens. The hotel has been the nostalgic rendezvous for those in the know for decades. If you can afford to, try and stay here or at least have a meal at one of several restaurants (the *Museum Coffee and Tea Corner* is great for snacks and tea). From B3200.

The Regent Cha Am Beach Resort, 849/21 Petkasem Road, Cha Am, ph 471 480, fax 471 492. 566 AC rooms/chalets, restaurants, pools, tennis, squash, gym, watersports, shops and nightclub. From B3000.

Local Transport

Local buses and *songthaews* travel the highway connecting both resorts. Fares range between B5 and B10. Irregular train services also connect the towns. Within the towns there are trishaw and motor bikes. Both resort towns are small enough to walk to any destinations.

Eating Out and Entertainment

Seafood, freshly caught in the Gulf of Thailand, features in most restaurants. If you don't believe it is fresh, wander down to the pier area and see the catches being landed. Some of the best and cheapest food in town is available in the markets where makeshift eating areas are established in the evening. There are a few restaurants lining the beach and actually extending over the beach (the *Meekaruna* is very good). Cheap Thai meals are prepared by stall holders along the beach, and they also rent out the deck chairs. The large hotels/resorts mostly have à la carte or theme night buffets, and welcome diners who are not staying in the hotel.

Some other places to try in Hua Hin include the following: *Angus Steak House* (yes, you guessed it, Australian steak), *White Lotus* (Cantonese food with a view on the top floor of the Melia Hotel) and *Sea Side* (seafood, besides the Melia Hotel). In addition to these, there are Australian, German Italian and English Pub bars/restaurants in town.

In Cha Am, try *Lomfang* (in the Regent Hotel), *Moomthip* (Thai seafood) and *Tappi Kaew* (Thai, seafood and Chinese).

Shopping

Pha phim khomaphat or khomaphat printed cotton is found in Hua Hin. Souvenirs made from seaside products like shells are available but in buying them you are encouraging exploitation of a valuable environmental resource. Don't buy them, shops will stop selling them and then we can all see them on the beach where they belong. Preserved seafood such as dried shrimps, squid and salted fish are popular with local visitors.

Sightseeing

Most visitors probably come to relax on the beach and play sports rather than sightsee, but there are some things in the province for those wanting to get out and about.

Cha Am
The main attraction in town is the beach. A former royal residence is nearby as is *Kaeng Krachan Dam*, 51km away.

Hua Hin
Klai Kangwon Palace, built in 1926, is located on the beach 3km north of the town. You can walk close to it but need a permit from the Royal Household Office to go inside. The royal family come here every summer.

Railway Station
As far as train stations go, this is quite an attraction and, for train buffs, worth visiting. There is a royal pavilion on the station where members of the royal family once waited for the train. Every so often, the *Eastern and Oriental Express* stops here and some hotels will organise buses to see it at the station.

Khao Takiap-Khao Krailat
Just 4km from town, these two hills provide a good view of the coastline, and for photographs are best visited in the early morning. There is a monastery on top of Khao Takiap.

Prachuap Khiri Khan
Just 12km from Prachuap Khiri Khan, lies Dan Sing Khon, a border town with Myanmar.

Khao Chongkrachok

The view from the hill over this coastal town, 320km south of Bangkok, is spectacular. There is a Buddhist monastery at the top of the 395 steps to the summit. The bay below has good beaches, some accommodation and is less developed than those in other parts of the province.

Khao Sam Roi Yot National Park

This park occupies more than 60km^2 of coast between Pran Buri and Prachuap. The park was the location for major scenes in the film *The Killing Fields*. Extensive wetlands form part of a bird sanctuary, which is home for many waterbirds. Caves, islands, escarpments and valleys are worth exploring. It is located on the coast 63km south of Hua Hin and features limestone mountains, caves (Keaw Cave, Sai and Phrayanakhon), floodplains, coastline and a few islands. The park is 33km by minibus from Pranburi Station. Accommodation should be booked by phoning (02) 579 0529.

Phetchaburi, Khao Luang Caves

They are located just outside town where the late morning and early afternoon light illuminates stalactites and Buddha images.

Phra Nakhon Khiri National Museum

Once a royal palace, the small mountain retreat 36km from Cha Am is now a museum open from 9am to 4pm every day and costs B10 to visit. The locals will know it as Khao Wang.

Khao Luang Cave, 5km from here, houses an important Buddha image.

Sports

Golf

Like in many areas of Thailand, golf has exploded in the region. Thailand's first golf course, *The Royal Hua Golf Course* (ph 512 475), was established opposite the train station in the 1920s. Other courses in the district include: *Palm Hills Golf and Country Club* (ph 520 800, Cha Am), *Springfield Royal Country Club* (ph 486 985, Cha Am), *Lakeview Golf Course* (ph 520 091, Cha Am) and *Cha Am Villa and Golf Club* (ph 471 974). Green fees start at B500 and golf clubs are available from pro shops at each course.

The South-East

Pattaya

Pattaya almost grew overnight when it was used for recreation by American soldiers during the Vietnam War. It is considered to be one of Asia's premier beach resorts, but many visitors will find that it is too commercial and the beach that attracts people is under serious environmental threat. Pattaya has a special charm that you either love or hate; there isn't much in between. It offers accommodation from the very best to the lowest dive, and all forms of entertainment from seedy strip joints to sophisticated drag reviews. The beach is jam-packed with semi-naked bodies soaking up the sun; you can almost smell the suntan lotion kilometres from the town. At night the reddened bodies move from the beaches to the bars and nightclubs. If you are looking for a traditional Thai cultural experience don't come to Pattaya as you will be disappointed.

Pattaya Festival in April, celebrates the attractions and events of Pattaya. Depending on your point of view, this is either a good or bad time to be in Pattaya; it gets very crowded.

The phone code number is 038.

How to Get There

Pattaya is 154km south-east of Bangkok. The only real option in getting there is by car or bus, both of which take between two to three hours. Buses leave the Eastern Terminal at Soi Ekamai (Soi 63) on Sukhumvit Rd, ph 392 2391 (AC) and 391 2504 (regular).

Thai Airways has a limousine service from Bangkok's International Airport to and from Pattaya, but it isn't cheap; (from B1,500). There is also a bus service at 9am, noon and 7pm which costs B200 per person. Tourists on a Pattaya package will probably have a connecting fare included.

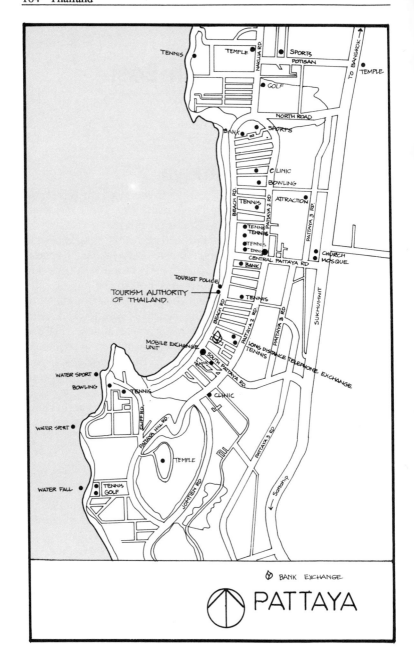

BANK EXCHANGE

PATTAYA

Bangkok Airways operates a daily Dash 8 flight from Koh Samui to U-Tapao leaving at 11am. The flight takes 50 minutes and a return flight to Koh Samui leaves at 12.20pm. Chartered flights often land at nearby U-Tapao. Helicopter charter from Bangkok airport to Pattaya is also possible. Some charter airlines now fly into U-Tapao.

Tourist Information

The TAT Office is at 241/1 Chaihat Road, South Pattaya 20260, ph 428 750, fax 429 113.

Accommodation

The general rule with Pattaya accommodation; the greater the distance from central Pattaya and the beach, and the fewer the facilities, the cheaper it will be. Such places also tend to be quieter and less glitzy, especially in terms of nightlife. Bang Saray is better if you do not like crowds, nightlife, shops and motorised watersports. On the other hand, if this is what you want, get as close to central Pattaya as you can.

Many big international and Thai hotel chains have hotels in the district. These include: *Asia, Dusit, Montien, Novotel* and *Royal Cliff. The Ambassador City Jomtien,* with over 5400 rooms, is the largest hotel in the world with facilities to match. It is popular for conventions and not the ideal location for a quiet romantic weekend. There are hundreds of places to choose from and it is difficult to make recommendations. Visitors should choose the hotel based upon the criteria previously mentioned. Some of them have great names such as; *Love Hotel, Peace Resort, P 72, Romeo Palace, Thank You Bingo, Freddie's Place, Mickey Mouse* and *Porn Guesthouse.* Guest houses can have rates as cheap as B100 while the resorts, in excess of B5000. TAT Offices can provide accurate prices and details. The following is a selection of places to stay. They are all located in Pattaya, unless otherwise stated.

Asia Pattaya, 352 Cliff Road, ph 428 602, fax 423 496. 320 AC rooms, restaurants, gym, bars, tennis, pool, disco and convention facilities. From B1800.

Cheer Inn. 87/41 Moo 9, Pattaya 3 Road, ph 428 998. 76 AC rooms, restaurant and bar. From B400. *Chottiwan,* 258 Moo 4, Sukhumvit Rd, ph 428 796. 12 rooms from B100.

Diamond Beach, 373/8 South Pattaya Beach Road, ph 429 885, fax 424 888. 138 AC rooms, restaurant, bar, gym, pool and shops. From B500.

Dusit Resort, 240/2 Pattaya Beach Road, ph 425 611, fax 428 239. 500 AC rooms, restaurant, bar, gym, golf, pool, disco and shops. From B2200.

Four J. Beach Resort, 69 Moo Jomtien Beach, ph 231 401. 85 AC rooms, restaurant and pool. From B400.

Jasmine, 547/34 Moo 10, South Pattaya. ph 424 591. 53 AC rooms with restaurant. From B250.

Merlin Pattaya, Pattaya Beach Resort, ph 428 755. 360 AC rooms, restaurant, bar, tennis and golf. From B1600.

Montien Pattaya, 369 Moo 9, Pratammak Rd, ph 426 502, fax 426 504. 320 AC rooms, restaurant, bar, pool and tennis. From B1800.

Noong Nooch Orchid Wonderland, Najomtien Road, Bang Saray, ph 429 342. 60 AC rooms, restaurant and pool. From B300.

Novotel Tropicana. 45 Beach Road, North Pattaya, ph 428 645, fax 423 031. 186 AC rooms, restaurant, bar, tennis, pool and shops. From B1300.

Ramada Pattaya Beach Resort, 144/81 Moo 10, Pattaya Beach Road, ph 428 755, fax 421 671. 325 AC rooms, restaurant, pool, tennis and golf. From B1600.

Royal Garden Resort, 218 Beach Road, ph 428 126, fax 429 926. 300 AC rooms, restaurant, bar, tennis, pool and shops. From B2000.

Royal Night, 362 Moo 9, Soi 5, Beach Road, 35 rooms from B350.

Sea Sand Club, Km 163, Sukhumvit Road, Bang Saray, south of Pattaya, ph 211 0632, fax 253 6178, 43 AC chalets, restaurant, bar tennis and pool. Although an old 'resort' it is pleasantly located on the waterfront near *Nong Nooch Village.* From B800.

Local Transport

As with all resorts, there are many options from self-drive to being driven. Around Pattaya, *songthaews* do regular circuits of the main destinations for B5 per trip. Other areas are negotiable and it is a good idea to ask an independent person before asking the driver. Destinations like Chonburi and Rayong are accessible by long distance buses.

Independent travellers can hire bicycles, motor bikes, jeeps and cars from the many outlets along the beach. Check the insurance conditions first.

Eating Out

Apart from good, but relatively expensive, Thai seafood, there are American, Chinese, Danish, English, French, German, Indian, International, Italian, Japanese, Korean, Mexican, Polynesian, Scandinavian, Swiss and Vietnamese restaurants. No doubt, a few nationalities have been missed. Pattaya has something for all tastes from authentic Thai food to that which will satisfy homesick tourists desiring food just like back home. Every fast food imaginable is available, as is halal food to cater to the large numbers of tourists from the Middle East.

There is great variety with seafood, naturally, featuring on most menus. Seafood is best along the southern end of Beach Road, It is expensive though, compared to other Thai destinations.

Entertainment

Most nightlife in the city revolves around girlie bars, nightclubs, kick-boxing, discos and male-dominated activities. It is like a Patpong Road by the sea in many parts of the town. Such establishments are mostly located along the beach and in South Pattaya. Don't wander around Pattaya at night with your pockets overflowing with cash as someone could lighten your load. It is best to leave your valuables in the hotel deposit box.

Shopping

Pattaya provides typical Thai beach resort shopping from street stalls selling rip-off designer label clothes, jewellery, electronics, beachwear, cheap tapes and handicrafts. The shops are open until quite late in the evening or early morning. There are other more up market stores. The Chiang Mai Night Market, similar to that in Chiang Mai, is located on North Pattaya Road.

Sightseeing

Most people visiting Pattaya are probably content with lying on the beach or around the pool. The main beaches are Pattaya Beach and Jomtien, (also spelt Chomthian) 4km to the south. The beaches and nightlife are the main attractions. There are some other places of interest including:

Elephant Village
If you must see animals do tricks, like play football, the Elephant Village is not far from town with showtime at 2.30pm.

Khao Khiew Open Zoo
This is a chance to see some Asian animals in near natural surroundings and without bars. Most of the animals are housed on islands surrounded by moats. Visitors can get close to many birds in the large walk-in aviary. There are simple bungalows and a restaurant. The zoo is south of Pattaya, ph 321 525.

Koh Larn
The main island off Pattaya is just 45 minutes by boat. As Pattaya became crowded, the crowds moved to Koh Larn. The attractions are more of the same; parasailing, diving, scuba, windsurfing and swimming in less congested conditions. Restaurants and deckchairs line the small beach. Round tickets cost B100 or B250 for ferry and lunch. You can also get to the island on sailing junks or charter them for several days of cruising the islands.

Mini Siam
Tourists who can't see the whole of Thailand, can see it in miniature in a few hours. It is located 3km from central Pattaya.

Nong Nooch Village
The village is on 250ha of landscaped gardens, 20 minutes south of Pattaya on the way to Bang Saray. It features orchids, arts, crafts, traditional dances and an elephant show. There are two cultural shows at10am and 2.30pm. Bungalow accommodation is available, ph 422 958.

Pattaya Park
This water amusement park is located on the beach, mid-way between Pattaya and Jomtien.

Wat Yansangwararam
Amidst all the resort attractions, *wats* appear somewhat out of place in Pattaya. This modern *wat* on the way to Bang Saray offers meditation classes.

Outlying Attractions

Bang Saen Beach
The Beach lies 45km north of Pattaya, towards Bangkok. Nearby, the *Marine Science Museum* in Srinakarinwirot University, has live marine specimens and displays. The *Nong Mon Market* is close by and is the place to buy fish and see a market in action. *Ocean World*, a water amusement park, is located here.

Bang Saray
This was once a quiet fishing village about 20 minutes drive south of Pattaya. Development is slowly encroaching upon the bay but it is still a pleasant retreat from the crowds of Pattaya.

Sport and Recreation

Car Racing
The Bira International Circuit is 14km south of Pattaya on the road to Rayong. Occasionally there are international bike and Formula Three races. You can become your own star and race on the track in your own car/bike for B500/two hours.

Diving
Diving is possible for most of the year in this sheltered bay, however the best times are from November to March. Koh Larn off the main beach is the most popular site. Wreck diving to see the *Petchbury Bremen* and others is a highlight. You can organise dives to more distant destinations like Koh Chang and Koh Samet from Pattaya. There are several diving operations in Pattaya but try: *The Scuba Professionals*, 1/1 Moo 3 Pattaya Naklua Road, ph 221 860, fax 221 618; or *Reef Divers*, Ocean View Hotel, Beach Road, ph 428 084.

Golf
Pattaya has several golf courses where equipment can be hired. *The Asia Hotel* has a 9-hole course for its guests. Others include: *Bangphra Course*, 45 Moo 6 Tambon Bang Phra, Amphoe Si Racha, ph 311 321.
Green Ways, Sukhumvit Rd, Banglamung Chonburi, ph 428 002.
Panya Resort Course, 502 Moo 1, Tambon Bangpra, Sriracha

Chonburi, ph 322 370.
Phlu Ta Luang (Royal Navy Golf Club), Sattahip, ph (02) 466 1180
(ext Sattahip 2217).
Siam Country Club, 50 Tambon Pong, Amphoe Bang Lamung, ph
428 002.

Watersports
In addition to diving and scuba, just about every watersport is
available in and around town - windsurfing, sailing *(Royal
Varuna Yacht Club*, ph 428 959 and *Sundowner Sailing Services)*, jet
skis, parasailing, game fishing and water skiing.

Rayong

The town is located one hour south-east of Pattaya (or 185km
from Bangkok) and is best known for its 100km of coastline, Ban
Phe fishing village, and as the port for accessing Samet Island.
The province is known for its fruit, and durians, mangosteens
and rambutans feature in the annual *Fruit Fair* held mid-year.

The *Sopha Botanical Gardens* near Ban Phe has many varieties
of trees and some historical houses.

Buses for the town leave every 30 minutes from the Eastern
Bus Terminal in Bangkok from 5am to 10pm. The trip takes three
hours and costs B90. Buses for Bangkok leave every hour from
7am to 8.30pm. *Silkair* from Singapore have regular flights to
Rayong, ph (038) 426 651 (Pattaya office). The phone code is 038.

Tourist Information
The TAT Office is at 300/77 Liang Muang Road, Amphoe
Muang, Rayong, ph 655 421, fax 655 422.

Accommodation
Rayong Resort, ph 651 000, has full resort facilities; *Asia Hotel*, ph
611 022, from B70; *Dream Hotel*, ph 614 620, from B150; *Melody
Hotel*, ph 681 015, from B550; and *Rayong Sea View* ph 611 364,
from B750.

Samet Island

The five islands in the Khao Laem Ya National Park are 30 minutes by ferry from Ban Phe village. This island is relatively isolated with some quiet beaches. Boats leave from Ban Phe regularly during sunlight hours (6am-5pm) and cost B30 one way. The trip takes 40 minutes. Some places to stay include: *Ao Nai* (from B200); *Samet Resort* (from B500); and *Pop Eye* (from B200).

Chanthaburi

The province, 290km south-east of Bangkok is known for its fruit, gemstones and seafood. Other attractions in the province include the *Underwater Archaeologist Museum*, located in Khai Noen Wong. It holds an extensive collection of objects retrieved from wrecks. And *Ocean Sea World*, at Pak Nam, 25km from Trat. This is where Humpbacked and Irrawaddy dolphins are bred, ph (039) 312 567. Places to stay include: *Chanthaburi* (ph 311 300, from B150), *Bankaew* (ph 312 507, from B280), and *Eastern* (ph 312 218, from B380).

Trat

The province, some 400km from Bangkok and 180km from Rayong, is Thailand's most easterly. Trat is famous for its fruit and the world famous *Tab Tim Siam* or Thai rubies. The province is well known for its beaches and islands off the coast. There are 52 main islands of which 47 are located within the Koh Chang Marine National Park. *Koh Chang (Elephant Island)* is mainly wilderness with most of the inhabitants engaged in fishing. *Hat Sai Khao* and *Klong Prao* are the most popular beaches on the west coast and accommodation is available from B75.

Waterfalls include *Ban Khlong Phrao*. Snorkelling is good off *Koh Yuak*.

Deluxe accommodation is available at *Rooks Koh Chang Resort* from B1500. *Coconut Beach Bungalows* on Laem Chaichet has rooms from B100. From Trat, there is a 15 minute songthaew ride to Laem Ngop Pier before the two hour boat trip to *Hat Sai Kaew*. The boat leaves at 3pm and costs B70.

Buses leave the Eastern Bus Terminal from 7am to 11pm and cost from B80 to B150. The trip takes about five hours. You can get into Cambodia from Ban Hat Lek but with the unrest there it is worth checking first with the authorities as it may be illegal. Gems (rubies and sapphires), many from Cambodia, are available at Bo Rai and Khao Saming but you need to know your gems or you could be ripped off.

The North

Chiang Mai

The city is one of Thailand's largest with a population of about half a million. It is known in the tourist brochures as the 'Rose of the North', but nobody seems to know why. It is also the nation's oldest; having been founded by King Mengrai in 1296 along the fertile valley of the Ping River at the base of Doi Suthep. Chiang Mai was once the capital of the Lanna Kingdom. The old city is a neat square bounded by moats and fortified gates. The Burmese controlled the city twice, the last time in 1775. The city was relatively isolated from Bangkok until the 1920s. It has many independent northern characteristics.

The climate is a lot milder than Bangkok and the central plains and the mountains north of Chiang Mai provide refreshing relief from the lowland heat. For this reason, it is considered Thailand's most livable city. The best time to visit is in the cooler months from December to February when you may need some warm clothing especially if you are trekking.

Only a decade ago, Chiang Mai developed as a mecca for young backpackers keen to walk the hills and learn about the various Tibeto-Burman hilltribe descendants. The night markets were the place to buy authentic textiles and the many handicrafts of these people. Times have changed and new tourists are also attracted to the north. International hotels have opened the way for mass tourism. Sadly, most of the goods in the markets are commercial replicas of the originals.

There are over 52 *wats* in Chiang Mai, many from the Lanna Kingdom. Several are worth visiting. In December, 1995 the city hosted the South-East Asian Games.

The telephone area code is 053.

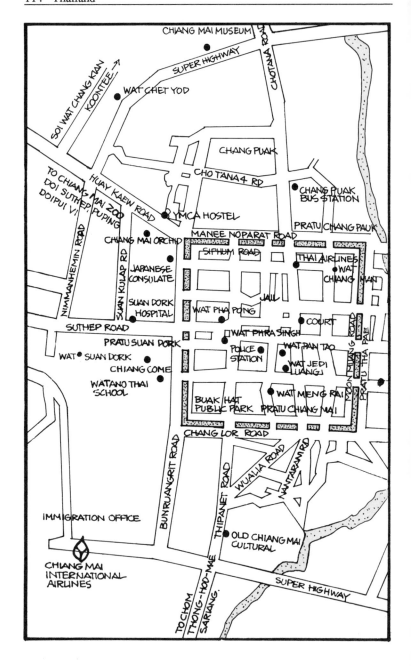

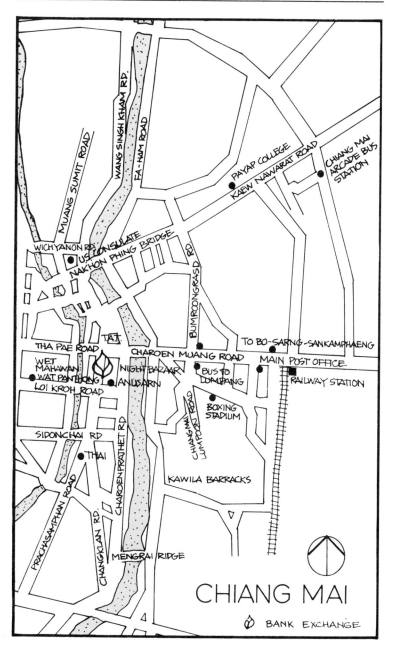

CHIANG MAI

◊ BANK EXCHANGE

How to Get There

By Air

Thai Airways (ph 210 042, airport 277 782) fly the one hour journey to Chiang Mai from Bangkok. There are about 10 daily flights from 7.10am to 10pm. *Thai Airways* flies from Chiang Mai to Chiang Rai, Mae Hong Son, Mae Sot, Nan and Phitsanulok. In the peak season, they have a direct flight to and from Phuket. The airport (ph 270 222) is 3km from the city and transfers cost B60 (taxi) and B40 (minibus).

Silkair flies direct from Singapore twice a week and

MAS (ph 02-263 0565), flies direct to and from Kuala Lumpur on Wed and Sun; the trip takes 2 hours 40 minutes.

Other international flights include: *Air Mandalay*, twice weekly flight to and from Mandalay in Myanmar (there have been some problems with passengers leaving and arriving in Mandalay and potential travellers had best check first) and *Yunnan Air* services to and from Kunming in China.

By Bus

AC buses leave and arrive in Chiang Mai from the Arcade Bus Station, Kaew Nawaratt Road (ph 242 664) and take nine hours to travel to and from Bangkok. They leave the Northern Bus Terminal on Phahonyothin Road in Bangkok (ph 279 4487 for AC buses, and 279 6222 for regular buses) regularly from 5.30am to 10pm and take 10 hours. AC buses cost between B270 to B370 and regular buses, B133.

By Rail

The journey is 760km and takes about 14 hours. Trains leave from Bangkok at 6.40am, 8.10am, 3pm (S), 6pm (S), 7.40pm (S) and 10pm (S) and to Bangkok at 6.35am, 3.30pm (S), 4.40pm (S), 7.50pm, 9.05pm (S) and 10.40pm (S). Those marked with 'S' have sleeping berths. The preferred night train to Chiang Mai is the 7.40pm and from Chiang Mai, the 9.05pm. These are faster due to less stops and arrive at appropriate times. However, you will not see any of the scenery on the way. The best day train from Bangkok is the 8.10am that arrives in Chiang Mai at 7pm. From Chiang Mai, the only train that travels all through the day is the

6.35am arriving Bangkok at 8.05. The Railway Station (ph 242 094) is not far from the town centre.

Tourist information

The TAT Office is at 105/1 Lamphun Road, Amphoe Muang, Chiang Mai, ph 241 466, fax 248 607. The office is worth visiting just to look at a traditional northern Thai teak house.

Accommodation

Superior Hotels

Amari Rincome. 301 Huay Kaew Road, ph 221 044, fax 221 915. 158 AC rooms, pool, satellite TV, IDD, pool, restaurants and tennis. From B2236.

Chiang Mai Orchid, 100 to 102 Huay Kaew Road, ph 222 091, fax 221 625. 267 AC rooms, satellite TV, IDD, disco, gym, pool and restaurant. From B2825.

Chiang Mai Plaza, 92 Sridonchai Road, ph 270 036, fax 272 230. 444 AC rooms, satellite TV, IDD, gym, pool, massage and restaurant. From B2200.

Diamond Riverside, 33/10 Charoen Prathet Rd, ph 270 081, fax 271 482. 321 AC rooms, satellite TV, mini-bar, IDD, gym, pool and restaurants (including Khantoke Dinner Theatre). From B2120.

Holiday Inn Green Hill, 24 Super Highway near Huay Kaew Road, ph 22 100, fax 221 602. 197 AC rooms, satellite TV, IDD, pool, gym, business centre and restaurant. From B2354.

Westin Chiangmai, 318/1 Chiangmai to Lamphun Road, ph 275 300, fax 275 299. 526 rooms overlooking the Ping River, AC, satellite TV, fitness centre, pool, sauna, restaurants (Chinese and Thai) and business centre. From B2400.

Standard Hotels

Chiang Mai President, 226 Vichayanon Road, ph 251 025, fax 251 032. 122 AC rooms, TV, pool and restaurant. From B820.

New Asia, 55 Ratchawongse Road, ph 235 288, fax 252 427. 240 AC rooms and restaurant. From B240.

Budget Hotels and Guest Houses

Camp of Troppo, 2 Charoonpathet Soi 4 Road, ph 276 457. B250.

Chiang Mai Travel Lodge, 18 Kampaengdin Rd, ph 271 1572. From B335.

Galare Guest House, 7 Chareonprathet Road, Lane 2, ph 273 885, fax 279 088. AC or fan rooms, overlooking the river, restaurant, and IDD in lobby. From B400.

Golden Inn Hotel, 470/23 Changklan Road, ph 274 550, fax 275 500. 64 rooms with a restaurant. From B300.

Green Lodge, 60 Charoenprathet Road, ph/fax 279 188. 24 rooms with AC or fan, bathroom, clean and close to the night markets. From B250.

International Hotel, 11 Sermsuk Road, Mengrairasmi, ph 221 820, fax 215 523. Comfortable, AC rooms with bathrooms, phone, restaurant, gift shop and tour agency. From B120.

Lanna Thai, 41/8 Loi Khrao Soi 6 Road, ph 282 421. 28 rooms with AC or fan. From B280.

Local Transport

Inner Chiang Mai is best walked especially if you are sightseeing. Buses and *songthaews* regularly travel around the streets. A *songthaew* from outside the airport will cost B20, substantially cheaper than the B100 asked at the terminal. Avis (ph 272 655) Hertz (ph 211 022) and Inthanon Tour (ph 212 373) provide rental car services; some of these phone numbers may be hotels; ask to be put through to the respective car company.

Eating Out

Khantoke dinner is popular in Chiang Mai. It includes a special meal and dance entertainment. The name comes from the wooden tray that the meals are served on. The main dishes are glutinous rice, Burmese and Northern Thai-styled curries, naem sausages, larb (spiced minced dishes), sauces, dips and crispy pork rind. For khantoke entertainment try: *Old Chiang Mai Cultural Centre* (ph 274 093), *Kan-Toke Chiang Mai* (ph 331 515), *Diamond Riverside* (ph 270 081) and *Lanna Kantoke*, located in a 150 years old teak house at the rear of the *Phet Ngam Hotel*.

If you would like to learn to cook Thai food as well as eat it, contact *Chiang Mai Cookery School*, ph 278 033. Local Chiang Mai dishes to try include naem sausages and khao soi noodles.

Antique House, 71 Charoen Prathet Road, ph 276 810. The Thai food is good and the setting is spectacular. It is located in a 100 years old teak mansion filled with antiques and flowers. The gardens are an ideal place to enjoy northern Thai specialities. They are open from 7.30am to midnight. The staff are friendly and helpful.

Galare Food Centre is located in Chang Khan Road, in the Night Markets. Here you buy coupons and take food from a series of stalls but the prices are not cheap. Indian vegetarian meals are available. Meals are written in English and there are pictures to assist. Refunds on unused coupons can only be redeemed on the same night.

Other places to try include the *Shere Shiraz*. 23-25 Soi 6, Charoen Prathet Road, just off the Night Markets, ph 276 132. It serves halal Indian, Pakistani, Arabic and Thai food. *Whole Earth Vegetarian Restaurant*, located in a transcendental centre near the intersection of Chang Klan Road and Si Donchai Road, has vegetarian Indian/Thai food that is good but a little expensive.

The fast food centre for Chiang Mai is the *Chiang Inn Plaza*. Here you can get *Burger King, Baskins, Mister Donut, KFC, Pizza Hut* and *Swensens*, assuming this is what you want. Just around the corner is a *7-11* Store.

Entertainment

Being a tourist town, there are many bars, karaoke lounges, clubs and discos. Some good places to start include the following:

Bubble Disco, in the *Pornping Tower Hotel*. Open from 8pm to 2am.
The Wall, in the *Chiang Inn Hotel and Lodge*. Pub, disco and live music from 6pm to 2am.

Shopping

Chiang Mai has always been a shopping haven for tourists. The Night Markets are particularly popular for hilltribe products and handicrafts that have been made in the district for centuries. These include antiques, silver jewellery, opium pipes, cotton products, laquerware and embroidery. It centres on Chang Klan Road although it spreads over the adjoining sois and roads. The main attractions are: *Tourist Mart, Chiang Inn Plaza* (has some smart shops including a Japanese bookshop and second hand books), *Sor Khan Kar* (stalls), and *Chiang Mai Night Bazaar* (stalls). *The Viang Ping Night Bazaar* that was once the mecca for hilltribe products is no more. It has been replaced by yet another hotel.

The road to Sankumpaeng was once lined with small artisans making their handicrafts. Catering to tourists is big business and factories have mostly replaced the small outlets. Still you can see the steps involved in making the handicrafts. Many places now have food outlets, toilets, offer free drinks and accept credit cards. Here are a selection of some of these outlets.

Bo Sang Umbrella Village. You can see the age old process of umbrella production. Traditional hand-painted paper, cotton and silk umbrellas are on sale. The village is 9km east of town. Overseas delivery can be arranged for large umbrellas.

Hill Tribe Products Promotion Centre, 21/17 Suthep Road, near *Wat Suan Dok,* ph 277 743 or opposite Chiang Mai University, has authentic hilltribe handicrafts. It is open daily 9am-5pm. All proceeds go to the Hill Tribe Welfare Program to establish an alternate source of income for people who normally grow opium and clear the forests. There is another outlet at the airport.

Pon Art Gallery, 35/3 Moo 3, Chiang Mai to Sankumpaeng Road, ph/fax 338 361. The rambling series of teak buildings house a vast collection of antiques. They have a showroom in *Chiang Mai Plaza* near the Night Markets.

Shinawatra Thai Silk, 145/1-2 Chiang Mai to Sankumpaeng Road, ph 338 053. Here you can see silk being woven as well as buy the finished products.

Silverware. There are many forms of silver jewellery available. Most of the retail shops are located on Wualai Road.

The Lost Heavens. 21 Nakornping Night Bazaar, Chang Klan Road, ph 274 823, fax 272 811. Open from 5pm to midnight. This stall in the Night Markets is more like a museum of Yao hilltribe pieces. Most pieces are collector's items to such an extent that few are priced. Serious collectors with money should visit and talk to the owner, Michael Goh.

Sightseeing

There are many things to see in and around Chiang Mai, most of them being ancient Buddhist *wats.* Much of the architecture here is a flamboyant mixture of Mon, Burmese, Sri Lankan and Lanna Thai styles. Many are adorned with woodcarvings, *naga* (snake-like) staircases, gilded umbrellas and temples featuring gold filigree.

Chiang Mai National Museum
Located on the Super Highway, next to *Wat Chet Yot*, the museum is closed on Mon and Tues. Opening hours are 9am-noon and 1-4pm. The museum houses Lanna works of art, ancient Buddha images and weapons.

Tribal Research Institute
The institute is located on the campus of the Chiang Mai University. Serious trekkers should visit the display and museum to learn more about the various hilltribes. It is open Mon-Fri, 8.30am-4.30pm.

Wat Chedi Luang
Built in 1391 and located on Phrapokklao Road, this is the site of the biggest pagoda in Chiang Mai. It was over 90m tall before an earthquake in 1545 destroyed much of it. It was reconstructed in 1994 at a cost of B35 million and *Wat Chiang Man* was used as a model. Many will not like the renovations as they are over-restored. For instance, only one of the elephant buttresses is original. The *naga* staircase, however, is particularly striking.

Wat Chet Yot
It is located just off the Super Highway, north of Doi Suthep-Nimmanhememin Road intersection. The temple dates to 1435 and contains a seven spire square *chedi* based upon one at Buddhagaya, the site of Buddha's enlightenment in northern India. It is partly covered in stucco which has been replaced over the years.

Wat Chiang Man
Situated on Ratchaphakkinai Road, the *wat*, dating from 1296, is Chiang Mai's oldest and was once the residence for King Mengrai. A *chedi* with elephant buttresses is interesting as are the massive teak columns inside the main chapel. *Phra Setangamani*, or the Crystal Buddha, is housed in one of the temples. It dates back 1800 years and came from Lopburi. It is only 15cm high and sits on a solid gold pedestal. This *wat* is being used as a model in the restoration of *Wat Chedi Luang*;

apparently there is a lot of guess work involved though. Like most of the temples, it is open daily 9am-5pm.

Wat Phra Sing

Located on Sam Lan Road, the original wooden temple has no metal nails, and dates to 1345. It houses the *Phra Buddha Sihingh* which is paraded through the streets of Chiang Mai every April during the Songkran Festival to encourage rain for the forthcoming rice crop. The murals inside the temple are being restored by the Department of Fine Arts. The ordination *wat* adjacent to the old *wat* has one side for women and one for male monks, so be careful which side you choose.

Wat Suan Dok

Situated on Suthep Road, the name means 'royal gardens' and it refers to the *chedis* containing the remains of members of the Lanna Royal Family. The family still exists and the last remains buried there were of two members killed in a disastrous *Lauda Air* crash north of Bangkok in the early 1990s. The *wat* was built in the 14th century and the bronze Buddha image, *Phra Chao Khao Ter*, is Lanna's finest. Although it is housed in an ordination hall, woman are allowed in as it hasn't always been used for this purpose. The large main *wat* contains beautiful timber beams and rafters. Interestingly, the tiles are dull brown and not the normal gleaming yellow green and orange. A Buddhist university is in the grounds which are next to a branch of *Hill Tribe Products.*

Zoo

The zoo is at 100 Huay Kaew Road, ph 221 179. Displays of rare barking and hog deer as well as other animals are found in this woodland setting 6km from town. There is a lake, *Huai Kaeo* waterfall, gardens, arboretum, and a jogging track adjoining the Chiang Mai University on one side and Doi Suthep-Pui National Park on the other.

Outlying Attractions

Chiang Dao Caves

The Buddha filled caves are 72km from Chiang Mai on the way

north to Fang.

Doi Inthanon National Park
Doi Inthanon, located in the park, is Thailand's highest mountain at 2565m. There are several spectacular waterfalls in the park including Mae Klang (58km from Chiang Mai), Wachirathan, Siriphum and Mae Pan. Tribal people still use the forests as do working elephants. There is an entry fee.

Doi Suthep
This spectacular temple, 16km west of the town, overlooks the Ping Valley. *Wat Phra That Doi* dating to 1383 is on the summit. The temple located in forests above the city is Chiang Mai's most important and visible landmark. It is 15km from town and over 1700m above sea level. The road to the summit is steep and circuitous. There are over 300 steps to be climbed after reaching the parking area and the ubiquitous souvenir markets. Alternatively, for B5 you can use the small funicular railway. The central pagoda of *Wat Phra That* is shimmering gold with a huge golden umbrella on each corner. The view of the Ping Valley on a clear day is impressive. However, on most days, the haze and pollution reduce this to limited visibility.

Elephant Training Schools
There are several schools in the north. Some are real schools but some are there solely for the tourists. At most, elephants demonstrate their skills in moving logs. At some schools they do 'tricks' that have little to do with forestry. On the Mae Rim to Samoeng Road, 10km from Chiang Mai, there is a popular school open 9.30-11am. Another school is at Mae Sa, 30km from the city. Admission is B40 and you can take a one hour elephant trek for B400 (ph 236 069). Other schools operate at Pong Yaeng Elephant Training Centre (Mae Rim to Samoeng Road, 19km from the city) and Chiang Dao Elephant Training Centre (on the Chiang Mai to Fang Road, 56km from the city, ph 215 787).

Mae Klang Falls
The falls are at the foot of Doi Inthanon National Park, 58km from town. It is pleasant for relaxing, picnicking and sightseeing.

Mae Ya Falls
The falls are located 12km from Chom Thom, on the way west from Chiang Mai to Mae Sariang. The drop and volume of the falls are spectacular. *Songthaews* from Chom Thom take 20 minutes. The falls are in Doi Inthanon National Park and the entry fee is B25. You can swim or just relax in the bamboo forest.

Obluang National Park
The park is 88km west of the city on the way to Mae Sariang. The 'Grand Canyon' where the Cham River is forced through a narrow gorge is exhilarating. Parts of *Tarzan*, the movie, were filmed here. Two kilometres from the gorge is the 'Cave of Prehistoric Man' where relics of previous human life were discovered.

Pa-Sang
Located 36km south of the city, Pa-Sang is known for its hand-woven cotton fabrics.

Phu Phing Palace
Beyond *Wat Doi Suthep* is the Royal Winter Palace constructed in 1962. It is open from Fri to Sun and on public holidays, except when the royal family are in residence. Nearby there is *Doi Oui Hmong Tribal Village*. It is a little commercial and set up for tourists who do not intend trekking.

Hilltribes and Trekking
Hilltribe people still attract many tourists to Chiang Mai as well as to Chiang Rai, Mae Hong Son, Pai and Mae Sariang. Treks to their villages are an exciting way to see the way of life of these people. Things are changing in the villages with many wanting the luxuries of life that go with development; TV antennas rising from thatched roofs are common sights in most villages. You need to travel long and hard to see a village that hasn't been 'discovered' by trekkers and trekking companies.

Major hilltribes include Lisu, Lahu, Hmong (Meo), Yao, Akha, Karen and Lawa. Their ancestors came from China, Myanmar and Lao PDR (a Karen elder, Poh Lei Pah, describes the journey as: *'travelling from the end of the sky to find a land of peace'*). The older tribes (Karen and Lawa) mainly settled in the valleys while the more recent arrivals occupy the mountain ridges. Today, there are estimated to be 500,000 in Thailand but many move across the national borders into neighbouring countries. Most are shifting cultivators who clear the forest to establish their crops.

Some of these tribespeople are animists and honour forest and guardian spirits; some are strong Christians while others are Buddhists. Most have distinctive courtship rituals, male and female roles, games, dances, music, puberty rites and languages or dialects. You need to consult your trek leader for the appropriate behaviour in each village as it will vary between tribes. In particular, spirit houses and gates at some villages must be left alone. Serious trekkers should go to the *Tribal Research Institute* at the University of Chiang Mai (open Mon-Fri, 8.30am-noon, 1-4pm). There are many books on the various tribes (*see section on Books, Films and Maps*).

Popular treks last from two to seven days and may include elephant riding (initially exciting but ultimately uncomfortable) and rafting. To access villages you may use a variety of transport but *songthaews* are the normal way. The cost of the trek will be determined by duration, distance, mode of transport and group size, among other criteria. For a guide, expect to pay about B1000/day. You will need to find out how much driving and how much trekking is done each day. Treks for Mae Hong Son that start in Chiang Mai, for instance, may require a long *songthaew* journey. It may be best to fly to Mae Hong Son and back and trek from there.

There is a romantic notion that all the hilltribes are drug-crazed natives getting out of it on opium. One of the attractions for tourists years ago was to see the opium business, from growing to consuming. The government is attempting to eradicate the poppy flower from which opium and heroin are derived. People who use opium, and it tends to be mostly older people, are a drain on the community as they have to be supported. You need to be aware that there are serious penalties for using such drugs. You may be offered opium; the decision to consume it is yours.

You should not take valuables while trekking especially in areas where there have been reports of banditry. Valuables should be left in a reputable safe deposit box. There are some stories of disreputable hotels using credit cards while people have been trekking; not a pleasant surprise when you get your next bank statement!

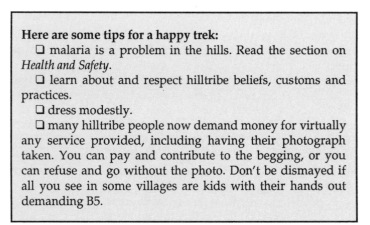

Here are some tips for a happy trek:
❑ malaria is a problem in the hills. Read the section on *Health and Safety*.
❑ learn about and respect hilltribe beliefs, customs and practices.
❑ dress modestly.
❑ many hilltribe people now demand money for virtually any service provided, including having their photograph taken. You can pay and contribute to the begging, or you can refuse and go without the photo. Don't be dismayed if all you see in some villages are kids with their hands out demanding B5.

It is best to shop around before going on a trek and ask people who have just returned from one. Trekking companies reserve the right to adjust their programs as conditions can change on the trek. Check to see what refunds are available should this happen. Some companies you could try in Chiang Mai include: *Lamthong Tour*, 77 Tape Street, ph 275 448; *Singha Tour*, 277 Tapae Road, ph 282 579; *Camp of Troppo*, 2 Charoenprathet Road, ph 279 360. *Skybird*, 92/3 Sridonchai Road, ph/fax 279 991.

For general travel agents try:
Chiang Mai Travel Centre, 301 Huay Kaew Road, ph 221 044; *Golden Tour*, 17/3 Charchprathet Road, ph 270 131; *Inthanon Tour*, 100/19 Huay Kaew Road, ph 212 373; and *World Travel Service*, 100/16 Huay Kaew Road, ph 221 044.

Tours
Details on organised tours of the city, neighbouring towns and the province are available from hotels, travel agents and TAT. These range from half day tours, to extended trips of one week's duration.

Lamphun

This small town, 26km south of Chiang Mai, is the former seat of the Hariphunchai Kingdom, and was established in 1663.

Wat Phra That Hariphunchai dating to 1157, is a classic example of northern Thai religious architecture. The temple is 46m high and has nine-tiered umbrellas made of gold. The site is worth visiting to see the variety of architectural styles in the various *wats* in the grounds. The *National Museum* is next door and houses many Lanna antiques. Like all museums it is closed on Monday and Tuesday. On other days it is open 9am-4pm. There are several other old *wats* in the town. Longans or *lam yai* are grown in the region and feature in a festival held in the town every August.

Lampang

The province and town of Lampang is located on the Wang River, 100km south-east of Chiang Mai. Trains and buses travel through here to the north, and the bus trip takes 1½ hours. There are two daily *Thai Air* flights, to and from Lampang and Bangkok (all flights go via Phitsanulok). Flights from Bangkok leave at 6.45am and 2.25pm while flights to Bangkok leave Lampang at 9.45am and 5.20pm. Temples worth visiting include *Wat Phra That Lampang Luang* and *Wat Phra Kaeo Don Tao* (Burmese influenced). There are caves, *Kui Lom Dam*, and a Young Elephant Training School in the district of Ban Pang La.

Pai

This is the sort of place where the police have nothing better to do than move sleeping dogs off the road. It was once just a village you passed through on the way to Mae Hong Son but it is quickly developing as a trekking and rafting town. The number of guest houses has increased dramatically over recent years.

Stay at *Charlie's House,* 9 Rungsiyanon Road, ph (053) 699 039, next to the markets on one side and the Krung Thai Bank on the other. Rooms start at B80 but the *'romantic house'* here, costs B200. Trekking has taken off around the town in a big way over

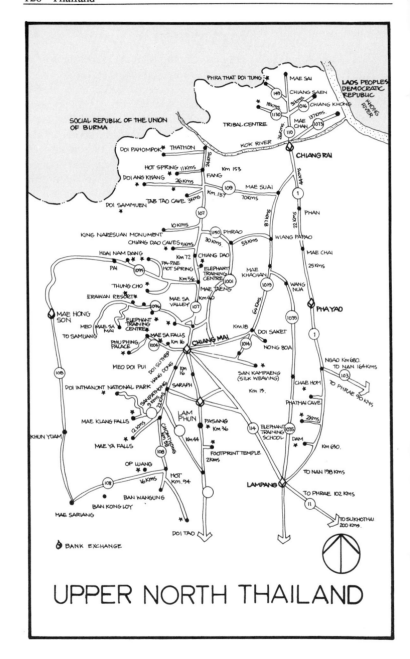

UPPER NORTH THAILAND

the past few years. From *Charlie's House*, they organise treks and rafting near the Burmese border. Around the town there are waterfalls (*Mae Yen* and *Mo Paeng*), hot springs (*Muang Paeng*, and *Pong Ron*), herbal saunas, temples and caves. Stopping in the small town makes a pleasant break in the long journey from Chiang Mai to Mae Hong Son. There are seven buses a day from Chiang Mai with the trip taking about three hours.

The place to eat both Western and Thai food is *Our Home Restaurant* where house specialities include tortillas, banana porridge, hoummos and pita bread. Needless to say it is packed with *farangs*. It also serves good Thai food. *Thai Yai Restaurant* around the corner is also good and for a drink, try *Pai's Corner Bar*. *The Lotus Guest House* has free accommodation if you enrol in their 'Lotus School of Culture' offering courses in traditional Thai massage, boxing and Thai cooking. You don't have to do all three but it is a challenge!

Mae Hong Son

The province is the smallest in the north and noted for its rugged mountainous scenery bordering Myanmar. If you want to see forested mountains and be far away from tourist crowds, this is the place. For most of the year, the hills surrounding this north-western town are covered in mist and the temperature is a lot cooler than the lowlands. This, and its proximity to Myanmar give the feeling of a distant mysterious land. Now that *Thai Air* flies to the town from Chiang Mai, five times/day (9.20am, 10.20am, 11.40am, 2pm and 4.20pm), Mae Hong Son is no longer such a mysterious destination. Return flights leave Mae Hong Son at 10.30am, 11.30am, 12.50pm, 3.10pm and 5.30pm. The journey takes 40 minutes and costs B345 one way. Flights into and out of Chiang Mai connect with Bangkok services. Alternatively, buses and cars take about eight hours depending on the route taken, either through Mae Sariang or Pai. Buses from Bangkok leave at 6pm and arrive 11am the next day. From Mae Hong Son they leave at 3pm and arrive Bangkok at 8am the next morning. It is 924km from Bangkok and 245km from Chiang Mai (via Pai).

The temples in the town are strongly influenced by Burmese architecture. The *Padong Karen* or Longneck People can be seen in Ban Nam Phiang Din and tours there cost B800. From an early age the woman place brass rings around their necks to enhance their beauty.

The telephone area code is 053.

Accommodation

Holiday Inn, 114/5-7 Khunlumpraphat Road, ph 611 390, fax 611 524. 2km from airport, alongside the Pai River. 114 rooms, mini-bar, satellite TV, IDD, restaurant, pool and gift shop. From B2000.

Mae Hong Son Resort. 24 Ban Huai Dua, ph 251 121, fax 251 135 (Chiang Mai Office). 53 AC rooms, bathrooms, IDD in lobby, restaurant overlooking the Pai River and pool. From B650 including breakfast. They also manage the newer *Riverside Hotel* next door.

Rim Nam Klang Doi Resort, 70/5 Khunlumpraphat Road, ph 612 142, fax 612 086. 39 AC or fan rooms, bathrooms, restaurant on the Pai River and IDD in lobby. From B500.

Don Guest House, 77/1 Khunlumpraphat Road, ph 611 362. Basic facilities from B50.

Sightseeing

Visit *Wat Phra That Doi Kong Mu* not for the Burmese temple which is nothing spectacular, but because the view over the town, airport and surrounding hills, makes it worth the effort. *Wat Young Kum* beside the lake is an interesting Burmese-style temple. The lake has been recently rejuvenated after being badly polluted. There are some pleasant guest houses around the lake (*Rim Nong, Jongkam Joe's* and *Johnnie House*). Other places of interest in the town and district include: *Wat Chong Klang, Wat Kam Ko, Wat Phra Non* (reclining Buddha), *Wat Kam Ko, Wat Hua Wiang, Pha Bong Hot Springs* and *Tham Lod Forest Park* (limestone cave), *Tham Pla* (Fish Cave) and *Ko Pang Waterfall*, 6km west of Pai. The Poi Sang Long Procession is a colourful Buddhist ordination festival staged in April.

Mae Hong Son is a popular trekking town. For information on treks of virtually any duration contact *Don Enterprises*, ph 612 236, fax 611 682. Their prices are slightly higher than other companies but they guarantee satisfaction. They visit Karen,

Shan, Kayah, Kayaw, Paku, Hmong and Padung (Longneck) villages. Their treks include elephants and rafting if required.

Khun Yuam

This is a small town with not much to offer except an escape from the larger settlements of the north. Few people stop here so it is also a nice escape from tourist crowds. The best time to be in this small town is November when the hills turn yellow with wild sunflowers.

Stay at *Ban Farang Guest House* on the northern side of town on the main road. There are 15 clean rooms from B40 to B200. Western and Thai food is served in the restaurant and they will organise treks, and motorbike hire.

Wat To Phae, 7km from the markets, is where teak tree rafts were once formed to take them to market. *Mae Surin Waterfall*, Thailand's tallest, is 30km north of Khun Yuam, but is only accessible in the dry weather.

Mae Sariang

There are a few Burmese style temples in this riverside town. These include *Wat Uttayanrom* and *Wat Si Bun Ruang*. Stay at *Riverside Guest House* beside the Yuam River at 85/1 Laeng Phanit Road, ph (053) 681 353 (eight basic rooms with shared bathroom, B60). Rooms in this teak house are good and the staff are helpful. They own a restaurant up the road and there is a beer garden below the guesthouse when the river is not in flood.

Doi Mae Ho, 25 km before the town, turns yellow with wild sunflowers in November and December. Access to *Mae Sam Laep*, on the Salween River, takes two dusty or boggy hours, depending on the season, from Mae Sariang. *Mae Surin Waterfall* in the Namtok Mea Surin National Park is the highest in Thailand.

Mae Sam Leap is a small market town on the Salween River that forms the border with Myanmar. While it is only 62km from Mae Sarieng, it can be a tortuous journey through mud, landslides and flooded streams in the rainy season or choking dust in the dry.

Chiang Rai

The province of Chiang Rai is about 11,500 km^2 with an average elevation of 580m so it tends to be cooler than the south. The capital, Chiang Rai, was founded in the 13th century and there are many archaeological sites to visit. The northern parts of the province border Lao PDR and Myanmar in what is labelled the Golden Triangle, and has been linked with the drug trade for decades. With the opening of Yunnan Province in China, the area is now promoted as the Golden Triangle. Chiang Rai is 785km north of Bangkok. It is the home of many hilltribe groups who live in the mountainous northern parts of the province. A visit to the *Hilltribe Museum and Handicrafts*, ph 713 410, is suggested for those who intend trekking amongst the hilltribes.

The telephone area code is 053.

Tourist Information

The TAT Office is at 448/16 Singhakhlai Road, Chiang Rai, ph 717 433, fax 717 434.

How to Get There

By Bus

Buses depart from the Northern Bus Terminal, ph 279 4484 (AC) and 271 0101 (regular). The journey is 875km from Bangkok and takes about ten hours. Local buses serve the province.

By Rail

Trains go to Chiang Mai; from there it is either a bus or plane to Chiang Rai.

By Air

Thai Airways, ph 793 048 (airport), 711 179 (city office) have up to five direct services a day, to and from Bangkok. There are another two flights a day from Chiang Mai.

By Boat

Many visitors to the capital arrive here by longtail boat from Tha

Thon on the Kok River. Depending on the weather and water depth, this journey takes from four to six hours.

Accommodation

Boonbundan Guest House, 1005/13 Jedyod Road, ph 717 040, fax 712 914. AC or fan, close to bus station, IDD in lobby, they can organise treks. From B100.

Dusit Island Resort, 1129 Kraisorasit Road, ph 715 777, fax 715 801. Located in the middle of the Kok River. Restaurant (roof top offering views of the city). From B2500.

Mon Rong Come, 339/1 Soi Homnuan, Phaholyothin Road, ph 716 371, fax 713 821. Modern AC huts with TV and phone or wooden bungalows with shower and phone.

Rama Hotel, 331/4 Trirat Road, ph 711 344. Located near the town centre next to *Wat Moon Muang.* From B180.

Wiang Inn, 893 Phaholyothin Road, ph 711 543, fax 711 877. International class hotel although a little old. It has AC, TV, fridge, restaurant and disco. From B600.

Sightseeing

Rafting
Rafting and longtail boats that leave Tha Thon frequently, end their five hour long journey at Chiang Rai.

Hilltribes
As in Chiang Mai Province, many hilltribes have made their home in the hills of the Golden Triangle. The Akha people, who live at altitudes above 1000m, are one of the most colourful.

Wat Phra Kaeo
This was once the original home of the Emerald Buddha now in the Royal Palace, Bangkok. It currently enshrines the Jade Buddha of Chiang Saen.

Golden Triangle - Chiang Saen

There is no real town called Golden Triangle, the nearest town is Chiang Saen, 12km to the east. (Chiang Saen is 60km from Chiang Rai.) The settlement at the Golden Triangle is called Sop Ruak. It is located at the confluence of the Sai and Mekong Rivers where Myanmar, Lao PDR and Thailand meet. There is a gateway proclaiming the Golden Triangle for tourists to pose under with Lisu girls (for a fee). Boats go to Kunming in Yunnan Province, China and Luang Prabang in Lao PDR (the latter being a five day trip). It won't be long before all four countries in the "quadrangle" open up. Somehow, the Golden Quadrangle doesn't have the same marketing ring as the Golden Triangle. There are current studies underway to connect the four countries by rail.

Chiang Saen is a 14th century town that contains several old *wats* in various stages of ruin or restoration, depending on how you look at it. Chieng Sean was once the home to Mengrai who became the King of the Lanna Kingdom. It was later occupied by the Burmese and much of it was destroyed in the 1700s when the Thais regained control.

The Buddha images and objects from the Lanna Kingdom in the Chiang Saen National Museum are worth seeing (open Mon, Wed, Thurs and Sat-Sun 9am-4pm). Other temples in the town include; *Wat Prathet Chedi Luang* (the 88m brick chedi remains complete), *Wat Pa Sak* (the stucco stupa is one of the finest in northern Thailand), and *Wat Phrathat Pha-Ngao* (4km to the east of town; the view from the hill across the town, Mekong River and Lao PDR, makes it worth the ascent).

Chiang Kong is a further 55km east of Chiang Saen and there are reports that tourists can get into Lao PDR for one day for $10. Other reports suggest that for B200, a 15 day Lao PDR visa can be arranged here.

Places to stay include: *Le Meridien Baan Boran*, Golden Triangle, Chiang Saen, ph (053) 784 084, fax (053) 784 090. 115 AC rooms, satellite TV, IDD, pool, restaurant, gift shop and soft adventure tours. From B1600. In Chiang Saen try *Gin's Guest House* and *Chiang Saen Guest House*, both in the B200 range.

Mae Sai-Tachilek (Myanmar)

This small town, 63km from Chiang Rai, borders Myanmar. It is now possible to get into Myanmar from here on a daily basis although this could have changed. Until recently, only Thai and Myanmar nationals could cross the river at the border. Foreigners could walk as close as they liked, only to be turned back by border soldiers. The Myanmar officials now request US$5 (they will not accept baht) and three photocopies that show your details and Thai visa stamp. You hand the copies in and nothing is entered into your passport (bad luck for passport stamp collectors). You can wander around the small market town on the Myanmar side until 5pm when you return and collect your passport. Here Shan horseman also load and unload their pack ponies for journeys back into the hills. There are many stalls selling animal products such as elephant tusks, bear paws, deer horns and various skulls. Chinese beer is well priced at B15/large bottle.

Travel agencies in Mae Sai also handle the paperwork for people wanting to do extended travel to Kengtung (also spelt Kyaing Tong) in the Shan State of Myanmar (you may be required to change US$100 into kyats for spending in Myanmar). Kengtung, 170km north of Mae Sai, is the unofficial 'capital of opium' and has been closed to outsiders for over 40 years.

On the way to Mae Sai there are turn-offs to *Doi Tung*, a mountain retreat 17km off the highway, and *Tham Pha Chom*, *Tham Phayanak* and *That Pum-Tham Pla*, all limestone caves.

Mae Salong (also know as Ban Santikeeree or Ban Santikiri)

Located high in the mountains of north-west Chiang Mai Province, Mae Salong is popular for local tourists especially in winter (December-January) when the blossoming Japanese sakura flowers turn the hills pink. The originals settlers were Chinese Kuomintang troops fleeing from communism in 1949.

It is a steep 42km climb from Mae Cham that is too difficult for large tour buses, so may save the town from mass tourism. The town is known as a 'high-altitude Chinatown' because of the Chinese herbal medicines available. Akha hilltribe woman also come to the town early in the morning to sell their produce. You have to be quick though as the markets are mostly over by 7am and the woman are very camera shy.

Places to stay include: *Mae Salong Resort*, ph (053) 765 014, fax (053) 765 135. 77 rooms have TV, phones, fridge and views overlooking the valley although many look like boxes with few windows. Rooms start at B500. The *Sakura Restaurant* serves good Yunnanese food although it is not cheap. The gardens and Chinese pavilions are very pleasant.

Gold Dragon Guest House, 13/4 Ban Santikeeree, ph (053) 765 009. It has several bungalows overlooking a valley. They have bathrooms with hot water, fireplace and restaurant attached. From B200.

Maesalong Resort, ph (053) 765 014, fax (053) 765 135. From B500.

There are several tea plantations clinging to the steep slopes around the town. There is also a mosque used by Chinese Moslems. The town is small enough to walk around the narrow streets that traverse the mountain ridges. In the town there are some very interesting characters including Buddhist monks, Akha hilltribe people and Yunnanese Chinese. The medicine shops contain traditional Chinese herbs, spices and probably several parts of endangered species.

Sukhothai

Located 350km north of Bangkok, this was Thailand's first capital, founded in the 13th century. The Kingdom is viewed by many Thais as the country's golden era when religion and architecture reached its pinnacle. The area was originally settled by the Khmers but the Thais drove them out in 1238. A city was established and Chinese artisans came to teach the art of pottery. Old Sangkhalok Pottery is eagerly sought by collectors. Replica pottery is made and sold outside the park.

The remains of this once grand city are preserved in the Sukothai Historical park some 12km from the town of Sukothai. The many temples within the 45km^2 landscaped park form a UNESCO World Heritage Site and recognise the regional and international significance of the site. The satellite towns of *Si Satchanalai* and *Kamphaeng Phet* are nearby. The *Loy Krathong Festival* held in November is particularly spectacular amidst the ruins of Sukothai. The *Ramkhamhaeng National Museum* has a large collection of Buddha images which can be seen Wed-Sun, 9am-4pm. The telephone area code is 055.

How to Get There

Until recently, there was no direct air link, as the nearest airport was at Phitsanulok, some 50km away. However, *Bangkok Airways* recently commenced flights directly to Sukothai. Buses regularly service the town from Bangkok in the south (ten times per day), Chiang Mai in the north and Phitsanulok to the east. The nearest train station is Phitsanulok and from here local buses make the 50km journey to Sukothai.

Accommodation

Pailyn, Charodvithithong Road, ph 613 310, fax 613 317. 238 AC rooms, restaurant, coffee shop and pool. From B1000.
Thai Village House, 214 Charodvithithong Road, ph 611 049, fax 612 583. 120 rooms and a restaurant. From B400.

Sightseeing

Sukothai Historical Park

The park is officially opened from 6am-6pm and fees are collected to see the 35 monuments during these hours. Inside royal palaces, temples, city gates, walls, moats and dams have been preserved by the Thai Fine Arts Department and UNESCO. The north-south walls are 2km long while the east-west are 1.6km. Bikes can be hired outside the park and they are the recommended mode of transportation unless you go on an organised bus trip. Serious temple visitors should allocate several days to see the sights in the park whereas the casual admirer may only last a few hours. To many, the park has been over-restored but it is still a very good place to see the Sukothai architectural style and the restoration works. There is a parkland feel to the site with its large lake in the middle. It is popular with Thais who picnic in the grounds.

Some of the leading temples in the park include: *Wat Mahathat* (13th century and the largest in the city, located in its centre with distinctive Sukothai lotus-style chedi); *Wat Si Sawai* (a three-prang *wat* which was perhaps once a Hindu shrine and later converted to Buddhism); and *Wat Traphanh Ngoen* (good view of other monuments from this location).

There are also several monuments outside the city walls. These include the remains of a celadon factory (the famous pottery from the district).

Phitsanulok

For most tourists, Phitsanulok will merely be a transit point for Sukothai. However, there are many attractions that make a stop here very rewarding. The town goes back to the Ayutthaya period when Phitsanulok became the capital for some time due to its strategic position.

Wat Phra Si Rattana, by the river, houses one of Thailand's most beautiful Buddhist relics, *Phra Buddha Chinnarat*. This seated Buddha dates to 1357. The *Museum of Thai Folk Crafts* records the local people's way of life (cooking utensils, farm tools and models of traditional Thai houses). The Nan River flowing through the city is lined with rusting house boats and floating restaurants. On the banks is a colourful night market.

While a new four lane highway is under construction to link Phitsanulok with Bangkok, in the city, trishaws are the favoured mode of transportation for locals. By bus, the city is only four hours from Bangkok. *Thai Airways* flies to Phitsanulok daily at 6.45am, 12.30pm, 2.25pm and 6.30pm. Return flights leave Phitsanulok at 10.55am, 4.15pm, 6.35pm and 8.10pm; the trip taking only 50 minutes. There are also flights to Chiang Mai, Lampang, Mae Sot and Nan.

The telephone area code is 055.

Tourist Information

The TAT Office is at 209/7-8 Surasi Trade Centre, Boromtrailokanat Road, Amphoe Muang, Phitsanulok, ph/fax 252 742.

Accommodation

Guest House, 99/9 Pra-Ong Dam Road, ph 259 970. 88 rooms with a coffee shop. From B200.

Phitsanulok Youth Hostelling International, 38 Sa Nam Bin Road, ph 242 060. An old wooden house surrounded by gardens. From B150.

Rajawong, 714 Mittraphap Road, ph/fax 259 569. 80 rooms, restaurant and coffee shop. From B120.

Wang Nam Yen Resort, Km 46, Phitsanulok to Lomsak Road, ph 243 124, fax 245 018. 35 AC rooms, restaurant, gym, pool and shop. From B1100.

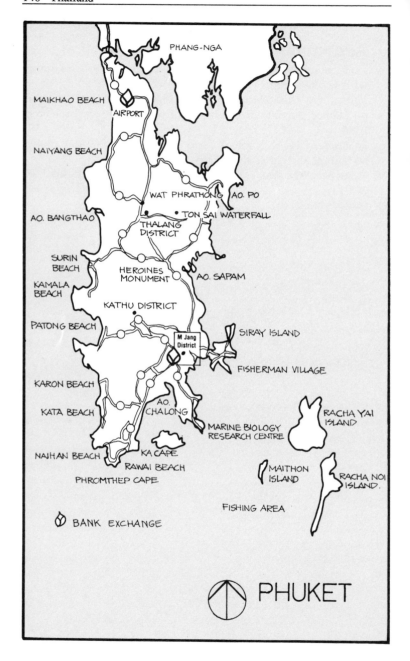

PHANG-NGA

MAIKHAO BEACH

AIRPORT

NAIYANG BEACH

WAT PHRATHONG   AO. PO

TON SAI WATERFALL

AO. BANGTHAO

THALANG
DISTRICT

SURIN
BEACH

HEROINES
MONUMENT   AO. SAPAM

KAMALA
BEACH

KATHU DISTRICT

PATONG BEACH

M Jang
District   SIRAY ISLAND

FISHERMAN VILLAGE

KARON BEACH

KATA BEACH   AO.
                 CHALONG   RACHA YAI
                                        ISLAND

MARINE BIOLOGY
RESEARCH CENTRE

NAIHAN BEACH   KA CAPE

RAWAI BEACH   MAITHON
PHROMTHEP CAPE   ISLAND   RACHA NOI
                                           ISLAND.

FISHING AREA

BANK EXCHANGE

PHUKET

The South

Phuket

Many parts of Phuket are tropical paradise and others are commercialised beach resorts not unlike those found in many other parts of the world. The island is located on the west coast of southern Thailand in the Andaman Sea. It is connected to the mainland by the Sarasin Bridge. Being 552 km^2, it is about the same size as Singapore. Most of the island is mountainous with tourist activities being concentrated in a few locations. About a third of the population is Muslim so you will notice a slight difference in the people and their customs in some areas.

It has been an important trading port throughout history predominantly for tin, pearls and rubber. The influence of Chinese traders is reflected in the architecture in Phuket Town.

Rubber *(Hevea brasiliensis)* was introduced to the island in the early 1900s. Now rubber trees are found all over the island. They are tapped early in the morning (3-10am) and then the liquid sap coagulates to form latex sheets that can be seen hanging and drying in the sun. Cashew nuts are another Phuket specialty crop. The best time to visit Phuket is out of the monsoon seasons (there are two monsoons in Phuket with May and October being the wettest months). November-February is the high tourism season. Discounted packages are available during the monsoon when the weather is fine between the storms.

Most national festivals are celebrated in Phuket but the Chinese Vegetarian Festival is specifically a Phuket event. It is celebrated in late September to early October depending on the moon. Devotees go on a nine day vegetarian fast to purify their minds and bodies. To help the process, some participants walk on hot coals and place sharp objects through various parts of their anatomy; a little like the Thaipusam Festival in Malaysia.

At many beaches you will find masseurs, food stalls, umbrella hire, and people selling a variety of goods from T-shirts to sarongs and drinks. In places like Patong, everybody is selling something. In the less established beaches you have the feeling of being on a deserted island.

Phuket is a real resort island with activities like shooting, horse riding, deep sea fishing, golf and even bungy jumping available. The telephone area code is 076.

How to Get There

By Air

Thai Airways (ph 211 195 or 212 400) has at least ten daily direct flights to Phuket from Bangkok between 7am and 9pm. The trip takes a little over one hour. There are flights from Phuket to Hat Yai, Nakhon Si Thammarat, Surat Thani, Narathiwat and Trang. *Bangkok Airways* (ph 225 033) has two daily flights to and from Koh Samui. These leave Koh Samui at 9.10am and 1.40pm, arriving in Phuket 40 minutes later. The return trips leave at 10.10am and 2.40pm.

You have to be careful on this flight as sometimes all your baggage may not travel with you if the plane, a *Dash 8*, is overloaded. Your baggage will arrive several hours later while you cool your heels in either Koh Samui or Phuket.

International flights also come from Penang, Kuala Lumpur, Singapore, Seoul, Hong Kong, Kaohsiung (and then to Taipei), Perth and Seoul. *Korean Airlines, Eva Air* (ph 327 507), *Pelangi Air, China Airlines* (ph 327 099), *Silkair* (ph 213 891), *Dragonair* (ph 215 734) and *Malaysian Airlines* (ph 216 675) service Phuket. Charter flights from *Lauda Air, Balair, Condor, LTU, Martinair, Scanair* and *AE* fly from Europe during the peak season.

The airport (ph 311 511) is 31km from Phuket Town and similar distances from beach resorts. It has an information counter, TAT desk, left-luggage counter, money exchange, post office, gift shops, first-aid, Muslim prayer room, restaurants and airline offices. Minibus transfers cost B100 to the beaches, B70 to Phuket Town, while limousines cost B400. Transfers to the airport leave from the *Thai Airways Office* in Phuket Town.

By Rail
There is no direct rail service to Phuket, and the nearest station is Surat Thani, six hours away.

By Bus
Regular bus services leave the Southern Bus Terminal for the 14 hour journey to Phuket. Buses from Singapore and Malaysia that overnight in Hat Yai, also service Phuket. Buses from Hat Yai take about seven hours. The bus terminal in Phuket Town is referred to as *Bor-kor-sor*. From here you can get a taxi to any beach destination for about B150. It is cheaper to go to the main markets (Talaat Sot), and get a local public bus for between B10 (Patong) to B20 (Nai Harn).

Tourist Information
The TAT Office is at 73-75 Phuket Road, Amphoe Muang, Phuket Town, ph 212 213, fax 213 582. Tourist Police can be reached on ph 212 468.

Accommodation
There is a wide variety of accommodation on the island with over 240 hotels and innumerable bungalows to choose from. Most people elect to stay near the beaches although there are some good hotels in the town. The prices of each hotel will give you an indication of the standards. They should be used as a guide as many offer packages that are substantially cheaper than the rack rate. For convenience, the accommodation has been listed according to the location. I suggest visitors choose the beach, and then the accommodation they can afford. Large hotels provide airport transfers.

Bangtao and Le Phang
The beach is 3km long with resorts and budget accommodation. The following hotels are integrated along the beach (Asia's first integrated resort); *Banyan Tree Phuket* (ph 324 374), *Laguna Beach Club* (ph 324 352), and *The Allamanda Phuket* (ph 324 359). There are many places to get away from the crowds. There are no hotels at Le Phang beach but there are food stalls.
Pacific Island Club. 323 Srisoonthorn Road, ph 324 352, fax 324

353. 253 AC rooms, satellite TV, IDD, a unique series of swimming pools, slides, restaurant, jacuzzi and a watersports centre in a rehabilitated tin mine. From B5125.

Sheraton Grande Laguna Beach Resort, Bang Tao Beach, ph 324 101, fax 324 108. 370 AC rooms, IDD, satellite TV, pool, tennis, golf, water sports and restaurants. From B4100.

Kamala

Casuarina and palm-lined beach with a coral reef a short distance offshore. It is just over a kilometre long and offers a quiet escape from the developed beaches. The accommodation is mainly bungalows and low-rise condominiums.

Karon

This is the next most popular beach after Patong. It is 2km long, peaceful and suitable for all watersports. There is little shade although planted palm trees are struggling to grow along the road that separates the beach from the hotels. It is about 20km from town. To the north of Karon is Karon Noi, a beach occupied entirely by *Le Meridien Hotel.*

Le Meridien Hotel, 8/5 Moo 1 Karon Noi Beach, ph 340 480, fax 340 479 (Bangkok 02-254 8147). 470 AC rooms, mini-bar, pool, gym, disco, four restaurants, tennis, squash, and watersports. From B3767.

Phuket Arcadia, 78/2 Patak Road, ph 396 038, fax 396 136. 475 AC rooms, satellite TV, IDD, restaurants and tennis. From B3550.

Kata and Kata Noi

Located 17km from town these two beaches, although some would say, one beach, are separated by a low hill. Kata Noi is located to the south and is smaller. Po Island sits off Kata beach. The beach is about 1.5km long with rolling waves.

Amari Kata Thani Resort, 3/24 Patak Road, Kata Noi Beach, ph 330 247, fax 330 426. 203 rooms/suites, TV, inhouse videos, IDD, mini-bar, several restaurants and bars, medical service and shops. From B2590.

Club Mediterranee, 7/3 Patak Road, ph 330 455, fax 330 461. 300 AC rooms, mini-bar, pool, snorkelling, wind surfing, gym scuba diving, tennis and disco. From B2600.

Laem Singh and Surin

Laem Singh beach is accessible by foot (ten minute walk from a car park) or by longtail boat. It is the next bay north from Kamala Beach, but about 4km by road. There is basically no development here except for stall owners seeking your food orders. There is no accommodation, just 250m of sand, forest and coral. Further north, Surin Beach, is better for surfing than swimming as the beach is sometimes dangerous.

There are many Thai-styled restaurants indicating it is popular with the locals. Accommodation is limited to budget chalets at either ends of the beach.

Surin Sweet Apartment, 107/5-6 Moo 3, Chengalay, ph/fax (01) 721 1153. 30 basic bungalows with restaurant. From B400.

Mai Khao

The northernmost beach on the west coast and seen by passengers flying into the airport. It is 14km long and mostly deserted. Hotel development is limited because the beach descends steeply into the water. However, the *Royal Gardens Group* is building a 155 room, low-rise resort.

Nai Harn

This is the location for people who like peace and quite. It used to be a backpackers paradise but authorities 'cleaned it up'. The beach, which is 18km from town, fronts onto a shallow lagoon protected by rocky headlands. It receives the full force of the monsoon and is best avoided during these months. There are few choices of accommodation apart from the ritzy *Phuket Yacht Club*, Nai Harn Beach (managed by the *Mandarin Oriental Resort Group*), ph 381 156, fax 396 038 (Bangkok 02-254 7091) which has one of the best locations on Phuket. The *Jungle Beach Resort*, is a bit further north and at B250 is good value. The *PYC* has everything that makes a real resort; it would want to at B7768.

Nai Thon

Isolated and difficult to access, but scenic and worth visiting.

Nai Yang

Mostly National Park covered in casuarina trees. The beach where the hotels are is good for safe swimming. There are bungalows for rent in the National Park, ph (02) 579 0529 (Bangkok). This is the beach to see turtles lay their eggs between October to February.

Crown Nai Yang Suite Hotel, 117 Naiyang Beach, Thalang, ph 327 420, fax 327 322. 96 all AC suite hotel, restaurants, satellite TV, IDD and pool. From B1250.

Pearl Village Hotel, Naiyang Beach, ph 327 006, fax 327 338. 226 AC rooms, satellite TV, IDD, 2 restaurants, tennis, pool, horse and elephant riding. From B3531.

National Park. Bungalows which sleep up to 10 for rent at B500. Tents are also available for rent at B60.

Pansea

The beach is only 250m long, with coral reefs and rocky outcrops, and is surrounded by forest. It is ideal for snorkelling, diving and fishing. The hotels are exclusive and secluded.

Amanpuri, 118/1 Pansea Beach, ph 324 333, fax 324 100 (Bangkok 02-250 0746). 40 exclusive AC bungalows, mini-bar, pool, tennis and restaurant. Entry is through *The Chedi Phuket* (formerly the *Pansea Hotel*). From B6900.

The Chedi Phuket, 118/3, Cheng Thalay, ph 324 017, fax 324 252. 110 AC rooms, satellite TV, IDD, restaurant, tennis and pool. From B3500.

Patong, Kalim and Nakalay

Patong Beach is the island's most developed, with shops, restaurants, bars and hotels as well as a pleasant beach. If you are looking for a holiday destination with a wide variety of facilities, this is the beach. If you want to get away from it all, don't come to Patong. Kalim Beach is the northern continuation of Patong and is a lot quieter. Further north around the bay is Nakalay Beach. All are about 20km from town.

Amari Coral Beach Resort, 104 Moo 4, Patong Beach, ph 321 106, fax 340 115. 200 AC rooms, satellite TV, inhouse movies, mini-bar, pools, jogging tracks, beach, bars and four restaurants and scuba centre. From B2900.

Club Andaman Beach Resort, 77/1 Thaveewong Road, ph 340 361, fax 340 527. 251 AC rooms, TV, mini-bar, pool, gym and restaurants. From B3708.

Diamond Cliff Resort, 61/9 Kalim Beach, ph 340 501, fax 340 507. Located on the hillside at Kalim Beach. 222 AC rooms, TV, mini-bar, pool, putting green, gym, tennis courts, business centre, restaurants and shopping arcade. From B3766.

Patong Resort, 94/2 Thawiwong Road, Patpong Beach, fax 340 541. 247 rooms, AC, satellite TV, IDD, 2 pools, health club, five restaurants and tennis courts. The hotel has two wings, the Pavilion and the Garden. From B2500.

Thavorn Bay Resort, 6/2 Moo 6, ph 340 486, fax 340 384. 30 AC bungalows, pools, tennis, sauna, gym and restaurant, The resort occupies the whole beach with forest behind. From B2200.

Phuket Town

Visitors doing business, those with a passion for urban living and those who like Chinese influenced cities, will choose to stay in town. Most people come to Phuket for the beaches and stay as close as they can to one. If you have to stay in town the following are recommended:

Metropole, 1 Soi Surin, Montri Road, ph 251 402, fax 215 099. 248 rooms, AC, TV, mini-bar, pool and restaurants. From B2000.

Phuket Merlin, 158/1 Yaowarat Road, ph 212 866, fax 216 429. 180 rooms, AC, TV, mini-bar, pool, tennis, restaurant and disco. From B1236.

Sintawee, 85-91 Phang Nga Road, ph 211 186, fax 211 186. 266 rooms, AC, TV, mini-bar, pool, restaurant and disco. From B470.

Thavorn, 74 Rasada Road, ph 211 333, fax 215 559. 200 rooms, disco, coffee shop and bar. From B250.

Rawai

This is the southernmost beach on the eastern side and the one least frequented by foreigners. It is a long, narrow beach lined with casuarinas. Hae, Raya Yai and Kaew Islands are accessible from here.

Rawai Garden, 64 Moo 6, Vises Road, ph 381292. 8 bungalows, fan and restaurant. From B250.

East Coast

Most visitors to Phuket go to the west coast because of the fine sandy beaches. The east coast can be summed up as muddy with mangroves lining the shores. Laem Ka Beach is an exception and one that hasn't escaped the attention of the owners of *Phuket Island Resort*. Chalong Bay is the departure point for boats to Phi Phi Island, Coral Island, Mia Thon Island, Racha Islands and several dive locations. Yachts often moor here. Restaurants are popular at night time with bus groups.

Phuket Island Resort, Laem Ka Beach, ph 215 950, fax 381 018. 300 rooms, eight restaurants (French, Italian, Japanese, Chinese and Thai), tennis, pools, volleyball and indoor games. From B 2943.

Local Transport

Tuk tuks operate within Phuket Town, and around the island there are buses. Tuk tuks go further afield at negotiated rates. Most buses leave the markets on Ranong Road in Phuket Town every 30 minutes. Fares to most beaches are B10. Around the markets you will see all sorts of local transport, including some trishaws and motor cyclists wearing red vests with a number on it. They take people anywhere around town for about B10.

There are innumerable car, jeep and bike shops all over the island. You should check to see you are covered by insurance and who pays for any damage should you have an accident. Expect to pay between B700 to B1000 plus fuel and insurance for a car/jeep and between B150 to B250 per day for a bike. The roads are better developed than Koh Samui but for visitors, the traffic is never the same as back home, so you will need to exercise additional caution on the roads.

Eating Out

On Phuket you can choose from *Grillhutte, Austrian Food, Pavarotti's Italian, the Irish Bar, Pizzeria Napoli,* as well as fine Thai food. The international jet-setting community has discovered Phuket and finding good Thai food at some of the resort beaches is a little difficult, but it is there. You won't find too many locals eating there though, it's too expensive.

Phuket has an interesting mix of seafood, Thai cooking, halal Islamic food and Chinese cooking. You can get virtually anything here. Finding where the locals eat is not always easy but look for the Thai markets or bus stops, that's usually a good start. Stall food is available on most beaches where *gai yang* and a beer is not a bad way to watch the sunset. Chinese food is readily available in Phuket Town.

Here are some recommended restaurants with the location and style of food.

Kata/Karon
Al Dente (Italian, Pizza), *Den Danske Kro* (Scandinavian), *Hayashi* (Japanese), *Lemongrass* (Thai), *Old Siam* (Thai), *On The Rock* (seafood with a view), *Sala Thai* (Thai), *The Boathouse* (Thai seafood) and *The Terrace* (French, Italian, Thai seafood).

Phuket Town
Chiang Mai (Thai), *Jibi* (Japanese), *Mae Porn* (Thai), *Thai Naan* (Thai, Japanese and Chinese seafood) and *Tunk Ka Cafe* (Thai, International).

Patong
Baan Rim Pa (Thai, views), *Berliner Gasthaus* (German), *Chart House* (seafood, international), *Faulty Towers* (English pub food), *Hide-Away* (Thai, Western), *La Gritta*, in *Amari Beach Resort* (Italian), *Malee's Seafood* (seafood, Italian), *New Delhi* (Indian), *Restorante Capri Da Rico* (Italian), *Suan Nok* (Thai).

Nai Harn
Moorings, next to *Phuket Yacht Club* (Thai), *Quarter-deck*, Phuket Yacht Club (seafood).

Entertainment
Like the variety of food in town, you can be entertained in a myriad of ways from magic shows (*Banana Disco*), cabarets, discos, house-parties, go-go bars, massage parlours to girlie bars. Patong Beach is the best place to start. It must be challenging for bar owners to come up with an original name. Try; *Baby! Rock Hard A Go-Go, Cats Club, Casanova Karaoke, Extasy A Go-Go, No Bra Away Club and Young Shark*. These bars are not all girlie bars! There are also various cabarets.

Like most tourist destinations in Thailand there is a variety of entertainment outlets including *Phuket Orchid Garden and Thai Village*, with sword fighting, Thai boxing, classical dances and ceremonies. There is a tin mining exhibition, elephant performances and a working rubber plantation. It is located on Thepkasattri Road, ph 214 860. Shows are at 11am and 5.30pm.

Shopping

Ban Boran Textiles, 51 Yaowarat Road, Phuket Town, ph 211 563. Located near the markets, this small shop has some excellent hilltribe textiles from around Chiang Mai. If you are not going north, but want to buy some authentic textiles and jewellery, this is a good place to start shopping.

Sightseeing

Aquarium
The aquarium located in the National Biological Research Centre at Phanwa Cape has 50 observation tanks. It is open daily from 10am to 4pm and costs B10. There is a souvenir shop and cafe.

Butterfly Garden and Aquarium
The gardens are in a beautiful setting with thousands of live butterflies. Unusual insects and spiders are also housed here as well as aquarium fish and other marine life. It is 2km from Phuket Town at Moo-ban Samkong, ph 215 616. Open 9am-5pm.

Chinatown
The centre of Phuket Town is almost all Chinatown. It centres on Phang Nga, Deebuk, Yaowarat, Krabi and Thalang Roads. Walking is the best way to explore Chinatown.

Gibbon Rehabilitation Centre
You can see gibbons dressed up like circus animals in some bars or in a near natural state at the rehabilitation centre. The former is illegal, and the latter, a far more pleasurable experience. It is located at the north-east end of Phuket, ph 381 065 for details.

Marine Biological Research Station
Both fresh and saltwater fish are housed in the aquarium. They also have a turtle hatchery. Between November and February, turtles lay their eggs on Mai Khao Beach, 40km north-west of Phuket Town. The Research Station is open daily 10am-4pm and entry costs B10, ph 391 126.

Markets, Ranong Road, Phuket Town
Phuket's morning markets are as lively as any in the country

except there is a strong Chinese influence. The shopfronts are very Chinese as are many of the products. The bus terminal is at the markets, so it is easy to find.

Naga Pearl Farm Island
Daily pearl-culturing demonstrations are held from 9am to 3.30pm. Boats leave from Ao Po for the island at 10.30am daily. A visit and lunch package costs B600. You can stay overnight in their bungalows, ph 212 901, ext 117.

Pa Pra Taew National Park
Most of Phuket's endemic rainforest has been replaced by rubber trees, but there are still some remnant stands. Pa Pra Taew supports palms, lianas and other tropical plants.

Rang Hill
If you want to look over Phuket Town, this is the place to go. The shade trees in the park make it a good spot for a picnic.

Rawai Beach
Descendants of the 'sea gypsies' still live in this village, 17km from town. It is a pleasant casuarina-lined beach with several accessible islands lying offshore.

Wat Phra Thong
This is also known as Golden Buddha Monastery. It is located at Thalang and has a large protruding Buddha image. Legend has it—people who try to take the gold image, meet with death.

Tours
Half and full days tours are available from the tour desks of large hotels. Smaller destinations will use AC mini-buses while larger buses are used for more popular tours. Here is a sample.

Phuket Tour (Rang Hill, Marine Research Station, Rawai Beach and Promthep Cape, half day, from B500).

Phang Nga Tour (James Bond Island, seafood lunch at Muslim village and temple visit, full day, from B500).

Phi Phi Island (boat trip, Viking Cave, seafood lunch and swimming, full day, from B650).

Pearl Farm (Naga Noi Oyster Farm, seafood lunch and

swimming, full day, from B500).

Eco-Nature Tours (ph 213 881, fax 210 972) offer 4WD rainforest and coastal adventures around Phuket and Krabi.

Sport and Recreation

If you haven't had enough with para-sailing, hobie cats, windsurfing and jet cats, then there's even more.

Bungy Jumping

Tarzan's Jungle Jump is open daily 9am-6pm.

All 50m jumps are insured, which must be a comfort if the band breaks, ph (01) 723 1123.

Diving

It is possible to dive Phuket from both the Andaman Sea and the Gulf of Thailand, ensuring year-round diving. The popular beaches of Patong, Relax Bay, Karon and Kata, have dive schools. There are at least 17 dive schools on the island, here are some; *Fantasea Divers*, 93/58 Moo 4 Thaaveewong Rd, Patong, ph 321 309, fax 340 309, *Marina Divers*, ph 330 625, and *Kon-Tiki Diving School*, 66/3-65/1 Patak Rd, Karon Beach, ph/fax 330 048.

Phuket International Marathon

International runners descend upon Phuket in July.

Golf

There are several golf courses on the island with many people coming here specifically for the sport. Fees vary but expect to pay around B350 for nine holes, B90 (caddy), B300 (club rental) and B300 (club car). Try the following courses: *Phuket Century Country Club* (ph 321 933), *Banyan Tree Club* (ph 324 350), *Blue Canyon Country Club* (ph 327 440) and *Phuket Golf and Country Club* (ph 321 038).

Hash House Harriers

If you want to run and 'on, on' meet at the *Expat Hotel*, Patong, every Saturday at 3.30pm.

Sailing

The six day *King's Cup Regatta*, in early December, is one of the premiere lifestyle yachting events in Asia.

Sea Canoeing

With the increase in more environmentally-friendly tourism, sea canoeing is becoming more popular. *Sea Canoe Thailand*, ph 212 172, or write to Box 276 Phuket 83000, guides adventures to sea caves and on open ocean expeditions. Day trips around Phang Nga are from B2500.

Thai Boxing

Every Friday night at 8pm there are eight bouts at Sap Hin in Phuket Town.

Outlying Attractions

Phang Nga

The beautiful limestone islands around Southern Thailand are best at Phang Nga. Koh Ping Kan or James Bond Island (it was the backdrop in *The Man With The Golden Gun,* and more recently, Oliver Stone's movie, *Heaven and Earth)* is the main destination for Phuket day-trippers. You can go by bus and then longtail boat, or entirely by boat (the latter leaves from Ao Po). If you go on a package tour, you will probably have lunch at Koh Pannyi (Sea Gypsy Island), a village built on stilts over the water (don't ask where all the waste goes). If you like crowds, this is the place to be with up to 3000 people having lunch here.

The telephone area code is 076.

Places to stay include *Phang Nga Bay Resort* (ph 259 9393, from B900), *Lak Muang 1* (ph 411 125, from B110) and *Lak Muang 2* (ph 411 500, from B300).

Around Phuket there is **Koh Raya Yai**, an island to the south that has escaped the tourism boom, at least so far. There are a few bungalows on the island that are accessible by boats from Ao Chalong.

Krabi

Krabi Town is not very interesting as a destination, it is more an access point for the beaches located some 16km away. Krabi is 2½ hours' drive from Phuket, about 4 hours from Hat Yai and over 800km from Bangkok. The nearest airports are Phuket,

Surat Thani and Trang. The limestone crags are a beautiful backdrop to the beaches that, up until a few years ago, were deserted. They have been 'discovered' and large hotel chains are staking out their turf (and surf) even along beaches that are only accessible by boat. These isolated beaches include **Rai Ley**, **Ao Nang** and **Nam Mao**. There are a few dive shops at Ao Nang beach on the Andaman Sea. Koh Podak and Koh Gai, are 30 minutes off Ao Nang beach and are deserted, coral-fringed paradises. **Susan Hoi**, or shell cemetery is nearby and contains fossilised shells up to 75 million years old. The phone code 075

Accommodation

Ao Nang Villa. ph/fax 637 270. 76 AC chalets, restaurant, pool and bar. From B450.

Dusit Rayavadee, 67 Moo 5, Sai Thai-Susan Hoy Road, ph 620 740, fax 620 630. There are 100 all-suite, AC villas located on the popular, but secluded Phra Nang headland. It is only accessible by boat. There are two restaurants, pool, gym, jacuzzi, tennis and watersports. From B8987.

Sport and Recreation

Diving

Try *Krabi Coral Diving,* Krabi Resort, Ao Nang Beach, ph 612 161, fax 611 914, or *Seafan's Divers*, Ao Nang Beach, ph 612 173. Podak and Chicken island are good for reef diving and snorkelling. They are usually deserted and offer a good escape from the busier mainland.

Canoeing

Sea Canoe Krabi (ph 075-612 173) and *Krabi Canoe Tour* (ph 075-723 1128) operate out of Ao Nang Beach near Krabi. They visit limestone crags off the coast or go inland to see mangroves.

Outlying Attractions

Koh Lanta

These isolated islands are being slowly 'discovered', especially as nearby islands like Koh Phi Phi are becoming congested. It lies about three hours from Krabi by boat and 90 minutes from Koh Phi Phi. There is a variety of accommodation available on the island, along a long sandy beach. Many of the island inhabitants are Muslim fishing folk and respect should be shown for their religious and cultural values.

Phi Phi Islands

These beautiful islands are also spelt 'Pee Pee'. There is Phi Phi Don (big island) and Phi Phi Lay (small island). The islands are 40km south-west of Krabi and 40km south-east of Phuket, and are accessible from both by boat or the occasional seaplane. The islands are small and there are no vehicles. Accommodation is restricted to the larger island and is virtually impossible to book during the peak season of December-January when about 5000 people per day jam onto the island. There is one main beach on Phi Phi Lay; **Maya Bay**. **Viking Cave** is located in the latter as are numerous bamboo ladders used to reach the bird's nests that go into the soup of the same name. The original inhabitants, Muslim sea gipsies, still fish the surrounding waters. The calm waters in the bay make it ideal for all watersports. There are dive shops and game fishing facilities. Each year 300,000 people visit these small islands and there are concerns for the island's environment. Garbage disposal, sewage and water treatment are all problems. This is a good example of loving a resource to death as the problem is basically a human one; too many people wanting to do the same thing at the same time in a small place. One of the islands' big attractions, coral, is slowly being destroyed by visitors. One solution could be to move the people to Koh Lanta. But, does this mean Koh Lanta will end up like Koh Phi Phi?

During the season there are about ten boat trips to the islands daily. They won't go during the monsoon if the weather is too bad. Most boats leave between 8am and 9am returning between 3pm and 4pm. The trip takes a few hours, depending on the vessel. You can get to Phi Phi on the *King Cruiser* (ph 076-222 570) which seats 888 (a very lucky number for Chinese) people and has a few cabins. Another way is to go on the *Seatran Express* and board the *Pakarang* surface submarine to see the underwater world of Koh Phi Phi. The journey takes 50 minutes to the island

and an all day return package is normally sold, ph 211 809.

Accommodation is available in simple huts for B80, camping for B50, or in luxurious facilities. Some places to try include:

P.P. Charlie Beach Resort, ph (01) 723 0495. Fan, toilet, shower, beachfront and restaurant. From B500.

Pee Pee International Resort, ph (075) 214 297. 120 chalets, windsurfing, scuba, snorkelling and game fishing. From B1500.

Pee Pee Island Cabana, ph (075) 611 496. One of the island's oldest establishments with AC bungalows and restaurant. From B750.

Diving

Try *PP Scuba Dive Centre*, Koh Phi Phi, ph (01) 723 0627, or *Manta Diving* on the island.

Similian Islands

This group of isolated islands is located 90km north-west of Phuket in the Andaman Sea. There are nine islands surrounded by clear waters which make them popular for divers; the 'vis' is good, especially during the non-monsoon months from December to May. The islands themselves are not spectacular and there isn't much for the non-diver. Wildlife here receives some protection as the area is a national park, and the lack of good beaches tends to keep the hordes and resorts away. Boats leave from Phuket, Khuraburi and Thap Lamu. Boats to the Surin Islands also leave from all these destinations. *Songserm Travel* (ph 076-222 570) have day trips.

Satun-Tarutao Marine National Park

Satun province is the southernmost on the west coast. There is no real reason to visit here unless you are going to Langkawi Island (Malaysia) or Tarutao Marine National Park. Access to and from Malaysia is relatively easy by road and ferry. Ferries from Satun to Langkawi, off the Malaysian coast, leave at 10am, 1pm and 4pm. From Langkawi, they leave at 9am, noon and 3pm. The telephone area code is 074.

Places to stay include *Satun Thani* (no phone, from B100), *Slinda* (ph 711 115, from B130) and *Wangmai* (ph 711 607, from B300). There are 51 islands in the park, covering an area of 1500 km^2. Boats to the park leave from the port of Pak Bara, 60km north of Satun, and go to Tarutao, Adang and Lipe. They leave at 10.30am and 3pm, take 1½ hours (for speed boats) and cost B200. Ferries take about 3½ hours. Accommodation for 250 people is available on Tarutao for B70/person/night and camping is also allowed. They serve meals too. There are nature walks (69 species of birds live on the islands), jungle treks to waterfalls and *Taru Hill*, turtles and diving (you will need to bring diving gear, as none is available on the islands). Adang and Lipe are accessible from Tarutao for a return journey of B360. Food is limited on the island so if you have a mad desire for anything special, bring it with you. Chalet accommodation is available at *Lipe Resort* for B500. On the return journey the boats stops at *Koh Hin Ngam* so people can photograph its spectacular black pebble beach.

Satun Travel and Tours organise packages (accommodation, meals and transfers) to the park. The park is closed during the monsoon from mid May to October.

Narathiwat

The people living in the three provinces of Narathiwat, Yala and Pattani, near the Malaysian border, are predominantly Muslim. Mosques are therefore more dominant than *wats*, the food is more Malaysian, and Muslim customs dominate. Narathiwat town is a quiet backwater with few great sights unless you are interested in wandering around isolated fishing villages and near deserted beaches. Few foreigners venture this far south although *Thai Air* flies to and from the town via Phuket on Wed, Fri and Sun. The monsoon churns the waters a chocolate brown and deposits flotsam and jetsam from the South China Sea. The deserted beach may also be a littered garbage heap. Fishing boats standing on the beaches make good photographs. Near the town, the largest seated Buddha in Thailand sits on top of a small hill. Parts of the *Taskin Palace*, visited annually by the royal family, are open to the public.

The TAT Office is at 18 Asia Road, Sungai Golok, ph 612 126,

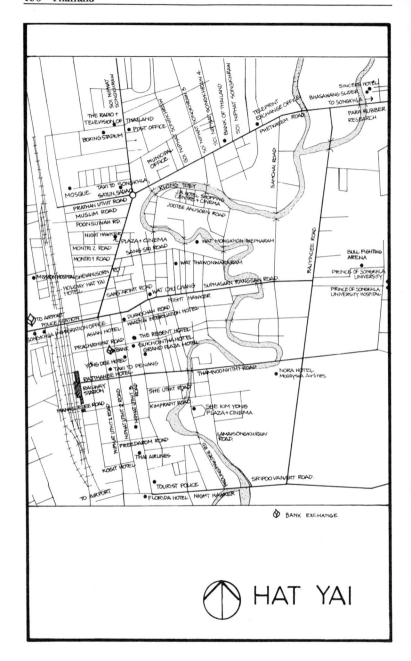

HAT YAI

BANK EXCHANGE

fax 615 230. The telephone area code is 073.

Most of the places to stay around this town and the town of Sungai Golok, on the Thai-Malaysian border, are simple, cheap hotels that are part of the prostitution industry flourishing along the border.

In Narathiwat try *Cathay* (ph 611 501, from B150) *Panan Resort* (ph 511 070, from B220) and *Tanyong* (ph 511 477, from B550). In Sungai Golok; *Merlin* (ph 611 030, from B230), *Asia* (ph 611 101, from B120), *Banggalo Golok* (ph 611 218, from B320) and *Genting* (ph 613 231, from B650).

Songkhla and Hat Yai

Hat Yai (sometimes spelt Haadyai) is located 950km from Bangkok in southern Thailand, just 50km from the Malaysian border. It is a thriving entertainment and shopping city, mainly for Malaysians. The night time entertainment is particularly attractive to Malaysian men. Bull fights, between bulls and not man and bull, are held on the first Sunday of the month.

Songkhla, although smaller than Hat Yai, is the provincial capital. It was once a medieval pirate town. Just 30 minutes away from Hat Yai, Songkhla is best known for its beaches, particularly Samila Beach (inclusive of a mermaid statue on a rock) close to town.

The fishing village of Khao Seng is worth visiting.

Accommodation is often difficult to find in both towns on the weekends because of the number of Malaysian visitors. Native cotton, *pha ko yo*, is sort after as are cashews, dried shrimps and other fish products.

The telephone area code is 074.

How to Get There

By Air

Hat Yai is 975km from Bangkok (1¼ hours flying time) and the airport is 13km from Hat Yai. Transfers cost B40 (bus) or B150 (taxi). There are five *Thai Air* flights per day to and from Bangkok. There are also three flights daily to and from Phuket.

Silkair (ph 238 901) fly daily from Singapore. *MAS* (ph 243

729) has daily flights (except Mon) to and from Hat Yai to Kuala Lumpur.

By Rail
The city is on the main north-south rail line and all trains stop here. There are several services a day to and from Bangkok, and daily trains to Butterworth (Malaysia), Kuala Lumpur and Singapore. Hat Yai is the train junction for trains travelling south-east to Yala and through to Sungai Golok for Kota Bahru in Malaysia.

By Bus
Hat Yai is three hours from Penang and nine hours from Kuala Lumpur.

Tourist Information
The TAT Office is at 1/1 Soi 2 Niphat Uthit 3 Road, Hat Yai, ph 243 747, fax 245 986.

Accommodation

Hat Yai
Ambassador, 23 Sriphadung-Phakdi Road, ph 234 410, fax 234 410. 170 AC rooms with restaurant. From B400.

Dusit J.B., 99 Juti-Anuson Road, ph 234 300, fax 243 499. 430 AC rooms with restaurant, pool and tennis. From B1600.

King's, 126 Niphat-Uthit Road, ph 234 966. 88 AC rooms with restaurant. From B250.

Metro, 86 Niphat-Uthit Road, ph 244 422. 155 AC rooms with coffee shop. From B170.

The Regency, 23 Prachathipat Road, ph 234 400. 190 AC rooms with restaurant, shops and business centre. From B720.

Songkhla
Royal Crown, 38 Saingam Road, ph 312 174. 52 AC rooms with restaurant. From B550.

Samila Beach, 1/11 Ratchadamonen Road, ph 311 310, fax 322 448. 75 rooms and bungalows with restaurant, golf course, pool and shop. From B650.

Shopping

Many tourists, especially Malaysians, come here to shop. Most shops are found along Niphat-Uthit 2 and 3 Roads, Sanehanuson Road and Plaza Market. In Songkhla you can see cotton weavers making *pha ko yo*. Most sell directly to the public.

Outlying Attractions

Songkhla Lake

Just north of Songkhla is Thailand's largest inland waterway. The Great Songkhla Lake, or Thale Sap, is 80km by 20km and is accessible from several points including Songkhla in the south and Phattalung in the north. *Khu Khut Waterfowl Park* on the southern part of the lake supports up to 140 resident and migratory bird species. The 520 km^2 park is one of the largest of its kind in Asia. The lake is best visited early morning or late evening, when the birds are most active and the sun is less harsh. Boats can be hired just north of Songkhla at Khu Khut village (kilometre marker 33). *Wat Pakho* is located on the lake.

Phattalung

The northern end of Lake Songkhla is accessible from Phattalung on the train line, 115km north of Hat Yai. *Nok Nam Thale Noi* Bird Park is a highlight for bird-watchers.

The telephone area code is 074.

There are not that many places to stay in town; an indication of how many travellers pass through. Try *Ho Fah* (ph 611 645, from B120) and *Thai* (ph 611 636, from B130).

Nakhon Si Thammarat

There are also many fine and non-tourist beaches located around the city which is 784km south of Bangkok. One of the oldest *wats* in the country, *Wat Phra Maha That*, is situated here. *Thai Air* flies to and from here on Mon, Wed, Thurs and Sat. Places to stay include: *Khanab Nam Diamond Cliff Resort* (ph 075-529 000), *Nai Phlao Bay Resort* (ph 075-529 039) and *Nakhon* (ph 075-356 318).

The TAT Office is at 1180 Bowon Bazaar, Ratchadamnoen Road, Amphoe Muang, Nakhon Si Thammarat, ph/fax 356 356.

Surat Thani

This is the largest province in southern Thailand, covering
12,800 km^2. It borders the Gulf of Thailand and has many
islands, the best known being Koh Samui, the country's second
largest island after Phuket. Most travellers will only pass
through here en route to Koh Samui or wait for trains to other
destinations. The telephone area code is 077.

How to Get There

By Air

Thai Air has daily flights to the city. Morning flights are either
6.55am or 10.35am, depending on the day, and afternoon flights
are at 6.55pm. Return trips from Surat Thani are at 8.55am,
12.35pm and 8.55pm. The flight takes a little over an hour. There
are also flights to and from Surat Thani and Nakhon Si
Thammarat and Phuket. Passengers going only to Koh Samui
are advised to fly directly to the island on *Bangkok Airways.*

By Rail

Surat Thani is a rail hub with nine daily trains from Bangkok,
and eight going north to Bangkok. The trip could take 13 hours,
depending on the type of train. The bad news is that most arrive
or leave at unacceptable hours. Overnight trains are the most
acceptable with the 6.30pm rapid sleeper (arrives Surat Thani
7.00am) or the 8.37pm rapid sleeper (arrives Bangkok 8.35am)
being the preferred trains. Combined rail, bus and ferry tickets
are sold for Koh Samui.

By Bus

Both AC and regular buses leave the Southern Bus Terminal on
Charansanitwong Road, ph 414 4978 (AC) and 411 0511 (regular)
at regular intervals for the 685km trip. Bus travel is quicker and
more flexible than trains.

Tourist Information

The TAT Office is at 5 Talat Mai Road, Ban Don, Amphoe

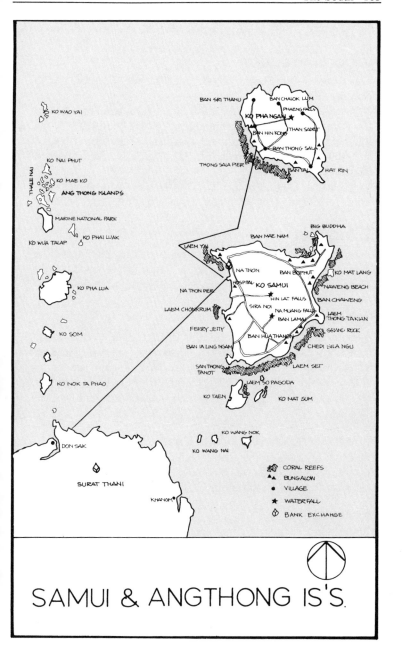

KO WAO YAI

KO NAI PHUT

THALE NAI

KO MAE KO

ANG THONG ISLANDS

MARINE NATIONAL PARK

KO WUA TALAP

KO PHAI LUAK

KO PHA LUA

KO SOM

KO NOK TA PHAO

BAN SRI THANU

BAN CHALOK LUM

PHAENG FALLS

KO PHA NGAN

THAN SADET

BAN HIN KONG

BAN THONG SALA

THONG SALA PIER

BAN TAI

HAT RIN

BIG BUDDHA

BAN MAE NAM

LAEM YAI

NA THON

BAN BOPHUT

KO MAT LANG

HOSPITAL

KO SAMUI

NAWENG BEACH

NA THON PIER

HIN LAT FALLS

BAN CHAWENG

LAEM CHONGKRUM

SIRA NOI

NA MUANG FALLS

LAEM THONG TAKIAN

BAN LAMAI

FERRY JETTY

BAN HUA THANON

GRAND ROCK

BAN TA LING NGAM

CHEDI SILA NGU

SAN THONG TANOT

LAEM SET

LAEM SO PAGODA

KO TAEN

KO MAT SUM

KO WANG NOK

KO WANG NAI

DON SAK

SURAT THANI

KHANOM

CORAL REEFS

BUNGALOW

VILLAGE

WATERFALL

BANK EXCHANGE

SAMUI & ANGTHONG IS'S.

Muang, Surat Thani. ph 281 828, fax 282 828.

Accommodation

Muang Thong, Na Muang Road, ph 272 960. 180 rooms with restaurant. From B130.

Rat Thani, 293 Talad Mai Rd, ph 272 972. 105 rooms. From B150.

Siam Thani, 180 Surat-Phunphin Rd, ph 271 0924, fax 282 169. 172 rooms with coffee shop, bar, pool, disco and shop. From B500.

Tapi, 100 Chonkasem Road, ph 272 575. 120 rooms with a restaurant. From B220.

Wang Thai, 1 Talad Road, ph 253 7947, fax 281 007. 230 AC rooms, restaurant, bar, pool, golf, disco and shop. From B600.

Eating Out

There are many good seafood restaurants along the Tapi River Estuary. The markets near the train station serve good, cheap Thai meals which are superior to the food found at the station.

Sightseeing

There is more to see around the district than in the town. Attractions include oyster farms, *Wipawadee Waterfall, Wat Khao Suwan Pradit* (mountain top temple), *Phra Borom That Chaiya* (1200-year-old *wat), Khao Sok National Park* (jungle, mountains, animals and waterfalls) and *Phumriang* (silver and gold brocade silk cloth).

Khao Tapet Nature and Wildlife Centre

The 210m high hill in the centre, 6km on the Surat-Nasarn Road, has a good view of the district. A *stupa, Si Surat Stupa* (or *Phra That Khao Tapet*) is on the summit. There is a guest house here.

Monkey School

Monkeys are trained to climb coconut trees and throw the nuts to the ground. It is 13 km on the Surat-Kanchanadit Road. Many places in the south have this 'entertainment'.

Wat Suan Mokkha Phalaram

The *wat,* 50km north of Surat Thani, is better known as *Suan Mok.* The monks here follow Buddha's earliest simple doctrine.

There is a back-to-basics approach to living, without the ornamentation of many other *wats*. The 60ha forest site has sculptures, and the spiritual theatre with its pictorial interpretation of Dharma is worth seeing.

Koh Samui

Once home to backpackers, Koh Samui has been 'discovered' by jet-setters. Located 84km east of Surat Thani, the island is only about 250km^2 but distances can be deceptive, for example it is about 30km from the ferry terminal to the main beach at Chawang. The cool season, from November to January is the best time to visit Koh Samui. The island is covered in coconuts palms which until tourism developed were the main money-spinner.

Angthong Marine National Park is located off Surat Thani and the corals are popular with day trippers and those wishing to stay in rudimentary accommodation. *Koh Tan* (Coral Island), 30 minutes to the south of Samui, is a less developed dive site. The telephone area code is 077.

How to Get There

By Air

Bangkok Airways flies to Koh Samui ten times a day from Bangkok (during the peak season, but less in the off peak), and the trip takes 60 to 80 minutes depending on the aircraft used. The first flight leaves Bangkok at 7.30am and the last one at 4.20pm. The airport on Koh Samui has been expanded to take larger planes. There is also a daily flight to Phuket and return which takes 40 minutes. Contact *Bangkok Airways* in Bangkok on ph 229 3454, fax 229 3450 for flight schedules. In Koh Samui contact ph 420 133, fax 421 489. *Thai Air* flies to Surat Thani three times per day on the mainland but then you have a two hour ferry trip. *Regionair* has direct charter flights from Singapore to Koh Samui. Enquiries can be made by ringing them in Singapore on 65-235 7808.

By Boat
Koh Samui is accessible by boat, speed boat or car ferry from Ban Don and Don Sak. Several companies operate this route. Combined rail, bus and ferry tickets use *Songserm Express* for the ferry component (ph Bangkok 252 5190, Surat Thani 286 340, Koh Samui 421 228 and Pha Ngan 377 046). Ferries can take up to two hours depending on the weather and passenger numbers.

By Rail
Although there is no direct train service to the island, combined train, bus and ferry tickets are sold by the rail authorities; enquire at any rail station.

Accommodation

Bophut
Boats to **Ko Pha Ngan** leave from this village on the north side of the island. The beach is long, the water clear and the setting tranquil. *IKK Bungalow*. Although their address is Chaweng Beach, they are about 3km from North Chaweng on the road to Big Buddha, ph 422 343, fax 422 482. This is one for those who want to get away from the crowds. The restaurant view over the forest and beaches is spectacular. Their own private beach is five minutes away. From B200.

Imperial Samui, Chawang Noi Beach, Bophut, ph 422 020, fax 421 397. 155 AC rooms, restaurant, bar, pool and shop. From B3300.

World Bungalow, ph 425 355, fax 422 355. 36 rooms, restaurant, bar, shop and pool. From B200.

Chaweng Beach
Chaweng Central is the hottest piece of real estate on the island, so the prices are the most expensive. As you move away from here, where the beach turns to former coral reefs, the prices get cheaper. If you are on a budget, stay at places like North Chaweng and walk the kilometre or so to the better beaches.

Amari Palm Reef Resort, ph 281 000, fax 282 001. 84 AC rooms and bungalows, TV, inhouse movies, IDD, mini-bar, restaurants, pool, jacuzzi, tennis, squash and water sports. From B1800.

Baan Samui Resort, 79 rooms, pool, *Moondance Restaurant*, satellite

TV and IDD. From B2400.

Marine Bungalows, ph 422 391. Simple bungalows with fan, bathroom and restaurant. From B150.

Moon Bungalow, North Chaweng Beach, ph 422 167, Simple bungalows on the beach—fan, toilets and restaurant. From B150.

Poppies Resort, 24 bungalows, Balinese pool, AC or fan, TV and minibar. From B5000.

Lamai Beach

This is the second most popular accommodation beach on Koh Samui, but it is less developed although this is changing. Lamai is more for budget travellers who are seeking a little action but without all the international facilities of Chaweng. Most places are in a thin strip that follows the coastline.

Aloha Resort, ph/fax 421 418. 26 rooms, restaurant, pool and shop. From B1200.

Best Resort, ph 421 416. 42 rooms, restaurant and games hall. From B350.

Casanova's Resort, ph 421 425. 20 rooms, restaurant, bar and pool. From B800.

Coconut Beach Bungalow. 19 rooms and restaurant. From B80.

The Pavilion Resort, ph/fax 421 420. 47 rooms, restaurant, bar, pool and shop. From B1600.

Other Beaches

The other beaches on Koh Samui are a little quieter although the general tone of the island is changing with the arrival of more tourists. On the north coast, places to stay include *Big Buddha*, *Mae Nam* and *Ko Fan*. On the west coast there are places like *Hat Thong Yang* and *Hat Ang Thong*. There are many other bays that are opening up.

Local Transport

Songthaew

There is a 50km ring road around the island. All destinations are regularly served by *songthaews* which have their destinations displayed. They mostly drive between two places, eg Na Thon to Chaweng. Most trips cost B15 to B25. They operate late evenings and early mornings for party-goers.

Car

Established car rental companies have offices on the island, *Hertz* for example, have a desk at the airport. Cheaper jeeps are available all over the island for about B800/day. Usually there is no insurance for these jeeps, you just pay for any damage. Accidents could make for a costly holiday so be careful.

Motor Bikes

The many scarred tourists and abundance of health clinics on the island should be taken as a sign for those unfamiliar with motorbikes. The roads are narrow with lots of things happening, so if you have not driven a bike before, learn before you get to Samui, or stick to sunbaking on the beach.

Nevertheless, bikes are a great way to see the country. There are bike shops everywhere and basic 100cc bikes hire for B150 per day plus petrol. Damage is your responsibility. You will be asked to surrender your passport or licence, which is never a good idea; give them something you can do without, should there be a problem.

Eating Out

Like Thailand's other popular tourist destinations - Bangkok, Pattaya, Chiang Mai and Phuket - Koh Samui has a good and extensive selection of restaurants. Many are located in the chalets and hotels that line the beach. Some of these are situated so close to the beach that you could be excused for thinking that you are actually in the water. Balmy evenings under the stars make these restaurants some of the most memorable of all meals in Thailand. While there are many good restaurants in the towns and shopping areas, they lack the ambience of those along the beaches. Every chalet, bungalow and hotel provides some form of meals, although some may only serve breakfast. The *Manohra Restaurant* provides classical Southern Thai dancing to accompany meals.

Sightseeing

Visitors to Koh Samui are more interested in the beach than anything else, but there are many sights on the island including a *Butterfly Park* and *Monkey Centre*. Other features include:

Waterfalls
Hin Lad and *Na Muang* falls are 3km and 17kms respectively from Na Thon. The freshwater streams make a pleasant change from the saltwater beaches.

Temples
Big Buddha (*Pra Buddha Kodom*), *Lam Sor Pagoda* and *Pra Tat Hin Ngu* are worth visiting.

Sport and Recreation

Diving
Snorkelling and scuba are popular around Koh Samui, Koh Pha-Ngan and Ang Thong National Marine Park. Dive shops can be found on the main Chawang Beach as well as Lamai and Big Buddha. There are about 14 dive schools in the district. Try the following; *Koh Samui Divers,* Chawang Beach, ph (077) 421 465 or *Pro Divers,* Lamai Beach.

Outlying Attractions

Koh Pha Ngan
Backpackers moved from Koh Samui as it was 'discovered'. The trouble for Thailand is there aren't many places left undiscovered. As soon as the word gets around people move on. *Koh Lanta* off Krabi will probably be the next big discovery. Koh Pha Ngan is a one hour ferry trip from Koh Samui. It is now a very cosmic place with lots of young people often dropping here for extended periods. Accommodation is mostly directed to budget travellers. The monthly New Moon parties are raved about by young travellers who flock to the island to indulge in hedonistic delights. The police are not always friendly to those who over-indulge.

Chumphon

This seaside resort town is located 470km from Bangkok. Arrival times of most trains are in the early hours of the morning so it is usually off the path of train travelling tourists. Places to stay include: *Jansom Chumphon* (ph 077-502 502), *Chumphon Cabana* (ph 077-501 990) and *Jane* (ph 077-541 330).

Koh Ngam Noi is a rocky island off the coast where bird nest collectors have huts.

The diving is reportedly good but still in its infancy, although there are a couple of operators in town.

Ranong

Ranong is 564km south of Bangkok and offers waterfalls, caves, forests and islands (Surin Islands National Park) in the Andaman Sea. There is also the popular *Jansom Thara Hot Spa Health Resort* (ph 077-821 611). Other places to stay include: *Asia* (ph 811 113), *Ranong Inn* (ph 077-821 523) and *Rattanasin* (ph 077-811 242). *Bangkok Airways* began flying to Ranong in late 1995.

The North-East

The north-east is the home of the Isan (sometimes spelt Esan) culture which dates back to the Bronze Age, 6000 year ago. The 17 province region is bounded by the Mekong River and Lao PDR to the north. The landscape is basically a vast plateau devoted to agriculture. To many Thais this is the real Thailand, the area where traditions are strongest and where many customs remain. The fairs and festivals of the north-east reflect these cultural traditions. These include the noisy Bun Bang Fai (Rocket Festival) and Khao Phansa (including the Candle Festival in Ubon Ratchathani). New destinations like Loei, Mukdahan and Nakhon Phanom near the Mekong River could soon provide further access into Lao PDR on the opposite banks of the river.

Nakhon Ratchasima

Nakhon Ratchasima, Thailand's seventh most populous city, is the capital of Thailand's second largest province. Otherwise known as Khorat, it lies 260km north-east of Bangkok.

Nakhorn Ratchasima is a thriving service town, transport centre and the gateway to north-east Thailand. The city provides access to various Khmer archaeological sites. For tourists who are not able to visit the great Cambodian temples at Angkor, those at Phimai and Prasat Hin Khao Phanom Rung in Buriram Province, are good substitutes. The telephone area code is 045.

How to Get There

By Air
Thai Air has daily flights (on Mon and Sat, there are two flights) to and from the city. The trip takes 30 minutes and costs B540.

Planes land at a military base ('the home of the tigers', so the welcoming sign says), and buses transfer passengers to the terminal off the base. Tuk tuk journeys to town cost B50 and take 10 minutes. *Thai Air*, ph 257 211 or 257 216 (airport).

By Rail
Trains to Nong Khai and Ubon Ratchathani service Nakhon Ratchasima. There are seven trains a day and the trip takes between five and six hours depending upon the type of train. The fare is B50 (Third Class) to B200 (First Class).

By Bus
Regular and AC buses depart from the North-Eastern Bus Terminal. Regular buses leave every 15 minutes throughout the day and cost B64, ph 271 0101. AC buses leave every 30 minutes between 4am and midnight and cost B115, ph 279 4484. The trip takes four hours.

Tourist Information
The TAT Office is at 2102-2104 Mittraphap Road, Amphoe Muang, Nakhon Ratchasima. ph 213 666, fax 213 667.

Accommodation
There are about 36 hotels, bungalow and guesthouses in and around the city. Here are some:

Chomsurang, 2701/1-2, Mahatthai Road, ph 257 088. There are 119 rooms, AC, restaurant, pool, disco and shops. From B750.

Doctor's House, 78 Supsiri Road, Soi 4, ph 255 846. There are only 6 rooms at this quiet and comfortable guesthouse. From B60.

First, 132-136 Burin Road, ph 255 203. 100 rooms with a restaurant. From B220.

Royal Plaza, 547 Chomsuraangyart Road, ph 254 127, fax 257 434. 150 rooms, AC, restaurant, bar and disco. From B700.

Siri, 688-690 Pho-Klang Road, ph 241 556. 60 rooms with a restaurant. From B120.

Local Transport
Buses leave for neighbouring towns and there are tuk tuks for getting around the town.

Eating Out

All the hotels in town have restaurants, and the stalls near the bus station serve reasonable food.

Sightseeing

Nakhon Ratchasima Craft Centre

Local silk, ceramics and plant products are available at the store behind the Provincial Hall.

Maha Weerawong Museum

The museum is near *Wat Sutchinda* and houses sandstone Buddhas from the Khmer and Ayutthaya periods. It is open Wed-Sun.

Pak Thong Chai Silk Village

Khorat silk is considered one of the finest in the land. The Silk and Cultural Centre is 31km south-west of the city. Visitors can see silk being woven as well as buy the finished material.

Prasat Hin Phanom Wan

This 12th century Khmer temple is smaller but similar to Phimai. It is half-way between Nakhon Ratchasima and Phimai You have to get off the bus at Ban Long Thong and it's a 6km *songthaew* ride to the temple.

Thao Suranari Monument

On the western side of town, at Chumphon Gate, stands a shrine to the local heroine, Khun Ying Mo. In 1826, she saved the city from Lao invaders.It is celebrated from late March to early April.

Wat Sala Noi

Located in the north-east of the town, this religious monument, in the shape of a Chinese junk, has received many architectural awards.

Phimai

The small town of Phimai has developed around a 12th century Khmer temple on the Mun River. The temple was once part of the Khmer civilisation centred in Angkor in Cambodia. Phimai was built in the late 10th century. If you can get to Angkor, do so to see the real thing. If you can't, Phimai is not too bad (if Walt Disney had been given the contract to construct Angkor, he would have built Phimai).

Prasat Hin Phimai is the central feature of the *Phimai Historical Park*. It is the largest sandstone sanctuary in Thailand. Much of the sandstone is pink, like *Banteay Srei* at Angkor. The other 'stone' is laterite, which is actually a soil that hardens on exposure to air. The fact that many stones do not actually fit, adds to the charm of the place. The temple has been restored, perhaps over-restored, and is now the main reason for visiting Phimai. It is very popular with Thais who come to have their photo taken in front of the 28m high *prang*. The park is open every day from 7.30am to 6pm and entry is B20 for foreigners.

There are other attractions in the town including the *Phimai National Museum* (6th century to 13th century Khmer artefacts) near the river (open Wed-Sun, 9am-4pm) and *Meru Bhromathat*, a pile of bricks near the town hall. The latter dates from the 18th century and was a cremation site. Out of town, there is a grove of banyan trees called *Sai Ngam* growing in a reservoir that is a popular picnic spot.

The annual Phimai Boat Races held during Loi Kratong Festival (October or November), attract many tourists.

Phimai is a very pleasant town and easy to walk around. The few places to stay include the *Phimai Hotel*, ph (044) 471 306, fax (044) 471 940, near the bus terminal (B160 for a room with a bathroom and fan), *Old Phimai Guesthouse* (214 Moo 1, Chomsudasadet Road, ph (044) 471 918, B80/room) and *S and P Guesthouse*, opposite. *The Bai Teiy Restaurant* is one of the few places to eat apart from the many small stalls.

Buses to Phimai leave from Nakhon Ratchasima central bus station (near Erewan Hospital) every 30 minutes during the day. The 60km journey could take 1½ hours depending on how many passengers it picks up. The cost is B16.

In nearby **Buriram** is *Prasat Hin Khao Phanom Rung Historic*

Park; a 10th century to 13th century Khmer temple situated on top of an extinct volcanic cone. *Prasat Hin Muang Tam*, an 11th century temple, is nearby. Both are accessible from Nakhon Ratchasima by taking the road to Surin and getting off at Ban Ta-Ko. The North-East Kite Festival held in Buriram in early December, is a good time to see *aek* kites fly (ancient yoke-shaped kites).

Khao Yai National Park

Located 200km from Bangkok, Khao Yai is one of Thailand's most famous national parks and covers an area of 2168 km2. It is mountainous with two major rivers, 20 waterfalls and many species of plants and animals.

Buses to the park leave from the North-Eastern Bus Terminal to Amphoe Pak Chong and from there local mini buses complete the journey. There are motels and bungalows available, but none are really cheap. Accommodation can be booked directly with TAT or through the National Parks Office in Bangkok (ph 579 0529). The park supports a great variety of protected wildlife including, tigers, elephants, deer, monkeys, bears, wild oxen and birds. There are also many species of rainforest trees, flowers and orchids. There is a good trail system providing access to the many wonders of the park. Night tours to see animals feeding at salt pans are also available. Many would argue that golf and national parks are incompatible activities but there is an 18-hole golf course in the park.

Khon Kaen

This city is in the centre of north-east Thailand, 450km from Bangkok. There probably isn't a good reason for stopping over here but if you are passing through, there is an excellent national museum that is worth visiting. Many pieces of artefacts from the Isan civilisation are housed here. These people once lead a nomadic life and evidence suggests they could have been one of the world's oldest agricultural societies. The displays at the museum have reconstructed this civilisation using remains from excavations throughout the district. There is pottery from Ban

Chiang, ceramics, bronze and old Buddha images. There are also displays of more recent village life and the utensils used by people in north-east Thailand. An excellent relief map shows all the archaeological sites in north-east Thailand.

The museum is open Wed-Sun, 9am-4pm and entry is B10. The museum is well signposted in English. It is only a 10 minute walk from the bus station.

Thai Air has four daily direct flights to and from the city. They leave Khon Kaen at 9am, 12.25pm, 5.20pm and 9.05pm.

Flights from Bangkok to the city leave at 7.15am, 10.40am, 3.35pm and 7.20pm.

Tourist Information

The TAT Office is at 15/5 Pracha Samoson Road, Tambon Nai Muang, Khon Kaen, ph (043) 244 498, fax (043) 244 497.

Udon Thani

The city is a junction for transport from Nakhon Ratchasima to Nong Khai, or from Loei to Nakhon Phanom. It is 560km from Bangkok. Apart from the airport (which serves the north-east, and Nong Khai in particular) it provides access to Ban Chiang. Ban Chiang, 56km to the east of Udon, contains remains of the Isan people dating back 6000 years. The excavations contain pottery, skeletons and tools. There is a small museum that is open Wed-Sun, 9am-4pm. The entry fee is B5.

Na Kha Village, 16km along the road to Nong Khai, is famous for its hand woven cloth called *khit*.

The telephone code is 042.

The airport at Udon Thani is a little out of town at the airbase that housed American bombers during the Vietnam war. There are 3 daily flights to the city from Bangkok. *Thai Air* office ph 246 697 or 246 567 (airport).

The TAT Office is located at The Provincial Education Office, Phosi Road, Amphoe Muang, Udon Thani, ph 241 968, fax 241 968.

Places to stay include: *Charoen* (ph 248 155, from B550), *Sri Chai* (ph 221 903, from B130) and *Udon* (ph 246 528, from B330).

Nong Khai

Nong Khai is the end of the north-east train line and a gateway for Lao PDR. With the opening of the Friendship Bridge across the Mekong, and the relaxation of entry requirements into Lao PDR, Nong Khai and Lao PDR will explode as tourist destinations in the next few years. One gets the impression that Thai commercialism will benefit most from the process and that Lao people will somehow get swamped or just carried along.

The main reason for coming to Nong Khai in the past was to look and ponder what went on in mysterious Lao PDR. Now you don't have to ponder any more, you can go and look for yourself. Locals on both sides of the river come and go as they please but for foreigners it is a different story.

Now there is a thriving business obtaining visas for foreigners to enter Tha Dua in Lao PDR. Visas cost about B2300 (B1800 in Bangkok) or over B3000 if you want it on the same day. If you are going to Cambodia first it would be advisable to obtain a visa there as it will only cost the equivalent of B250.

The Rocket Festival or *Bun Soeng Bang Fai* is celebrated at *Wat Pho Chai* in the second week of May. These elaborate rockets are fired to bring rain, thus symbolising the beginning of the rain and rice season.

The telephone area code is 043.

How to Get There

By Air

Thai Air flies to Udon Thani, 55km or one hour south of Nong Khai. They have a daily flights leaving Bangkok at 7am, 1.40pm and 5.45pm. Direct flights take one hour. Flights from Udon Thani leave at 9.05am, 3.45pm and 7.50pm. The fare is B1260 one way. The connecting bus from Nong Khai leaves two hours before the plane and costs B100; enquiries to *The Royal Express* ph 152 175 112 (*Thai Air* agents in Nong Khai).

By Rail

There are three trains a day from Bangkok to Nong Khai. The train leaving at 8.30pm and arriving Nong Khai at 7.30am the next morning has sleeping facilities. Trains from Nong Khai leave at 5.40pm, 7pm (sleeper) and 7.40am. A Second Class sleeper costs B450.

By Bus

Buses leave Bangkok's Northern Bus Terminal in the early morning or late evening. The journey is 616km from Bangkok and takes about nine hours. If you want to see other destinations in the north-east it is possible to use regular local buses between the various destinations.

Tourist Information

The TAT office is located at Salaprachakhom, Klang Muang Road, Amphoe Muang 40000, ph 244 498.

Accommodation

Facilities in the town are rapidly developing now that the Lao PDR link has opened. It could be said that Nong Khai has made it now that *Holiday Inn* is in town. There are a few small but good guest houses in town.

Banthoengchit, 626 Banthoengchit Road, ph 451 127. 24 rooms, restaurant and bar. From B80.

Holiday Inn Mekong Royal Nongkhai, 222 Jommanee Beach, Nong Khai 43000, ph 420,024, fax 421,280. 160 rooms and 38 AC superior, IDD, mini-bar, TV, videos, health club, pool, *Xanadu* disco, sauna, tennis courts, business centre, gift shop, conference facilities and restaurants. From B1800.

Mut Mee Guest House, 1111/4 Kaeworawat Road. They are proud of the fact they have no phone which adds to the tranquillity of the garden setting on the banks of the Mekong. It is in a little enclave that includes the: *Frontier Guesthouse, Wasambs Bookshop and Tai Chi* yoga and meditation centres. Rooms are B80/double with shared bathrooms. The food is good, the information excellent and the owners extremely friendly.

Nong Khai Grand Thani Hotel, 589 Mu 2, Nongkhai-Phan Phisai Road, ph 420 033, fax 412 026. There are 126 AC rooms, two restaurants, coffee shop, disco, pool, jogging track and business centre. From B1400.

Phanthavy Hotel, 1049 Hai Sok Road, ph 411 568, fax 411 567. 74 rooms with TV, fan or AC from B180. The *Udomrod Restaurant* downstairs serves good Thai food.

Local Transport

Motorised three-wheeled taxis (called *jumbos* in Lao PDR), pedalled tricycles and songthaews operate throughout the town; B10 will get you to most places.

Eating Out

Mut Mee Guest House serves good north-eastern Thai dishes in a garden setting by the river. You can also eat with the owners for B50 each night and have the dishes explained.

Songfangkong. This big restaurant has a pleasant setting over the river. Access is opposite the railway station to the west of town. There is a jet ski operation near the restaurant so if you are this way inclined, be the first among your friends to have jet-skied the Mekong.

Mekong Guest House, 815/1-3 Rimkong Road, ph 411 249, fax 420 967, west of the ferry terminal serves good food with great views over the river. They also have rooms at single B50, double B70, with shared bathrooms.

Sightseeing

Markets

There are several places to buy cheap goods. There are some Lao goods here but if you are going to Lao PDR, save it till then (try the Morning Market or Talaat Sao in Vientiene, which actually operates from 6am to 6pm). A temporary market has set up under the bridge on the banks, but whether this stays here remains to be seen. There are many shops along Rimkong Road near the ferry terminal.

River Cruise

Cruise the Mekong each evening, 5.30pm to 6.30pm to look more closely into Lao PDR and see the new Mittapheap or Friendship Bridge. The boats leaving from Tha Sadet Pier serve meals and drinks. The boat leaves from the riverbank near *Wat Hai Sok* and costs B20 for the cruise.

Village Weavers Handicrafts
Located on Prajak Road near *Wat Po Chai*, the village is both a showroom and demonstration centre. It features *mut mee* or indigo-dyed ikat cotton cloth.

Wat Hai Sok
Located on the banks of the Mekong, there are several religious buildings here, two are Buddhist and one Chinese.

Wat Khaek
Also known as *Wat Phuthamamakasamakhom*, it is about 4km from the city centre, and is not easy to find as the only sign is in Thai. About 1km from the edge of town, turn right after a 'children crossing' sign graphic. The road to the *wat* is 400m long and made from concrete. Firstly, this is not a real *wat* as it does not house monks and it features more than Buddhist images. This is one of the weirdest sights you will see in all of Thailand. The park is Thailand's answer to the Tiger Balm Gardens in Singapore and Hong Kong. It belongs to the creative imagination of Boun Leua Sourirat, a Lao artist and mystic who did things with concrete that construction workers only dream about. There are images from most traditional religions and a few extra constructed for good measure.

Don't try and work it out just go and marvel at the sight and the beautiful gardens, cacti and lily ponds. Entry is B5. If you are going to Lao you can see this *wat* with the one at *Wat Xieng Khuan*, almost immediately opposite *Wat Khaek* in Lao PDR. *Wat Xieng Khuan* or Buddha Park, is a similar collection of Boun Leua Sourirat's creations.

Other Attractions
In the province there are many other things to see and if you have time you should go to **Si Chiang Mai** (Vietnamese community), **Wat Hin Maak Peng** (meditation centre), **Wang Nam Mog Waterfall**, **Than Thong Waterfall** and **Phu Wua Wildlife Reserve**.

Nakhon Phanom

The town, on the banks of the Mekong River, is about as far east as Thailand goes, and is not to be confused with Nakhon Pathom near Bangkok. It is 735km north-east of Bangkok and the town of Thakaek in Lao PDR is opposite. There are several historic *wats* in town and waterfalls on the outskirts. There is an illuminated boat procession (similar to the Water Festival in Cambodia) and boat races during Ork Phansa Festival at the end of Buddhist Lent in late October. The telephone area code is 042.

The TAT Office is c/o City Hall, Aphiban Bancha Road, Amphoe Muang, Nakhon Phanom. ph 513 490, fax 513 492.

Buses leave from Bangkok's Northern Bus Terminal and take 7½ hours to reach the town. *Thai Air* has daily flights to the town via Sakon Nakhon.

Surin

Located 450km from Bangkok, near the Cambodian border, Surin comes alive for the annual Elephant Round Up. It is normally held in the third week of November. There are several elephant villages near the town. These include **Ban Ta Klang**, **Tambon Krapho** and **Amphoe Tha Tum**. The elephants are trained here by their mahouts.

Silverware is available in nearby **Ban Khwao Sinarin** and **Ban Chok**. **Ban Buthum** village on the road to **Sikhoraphum** produces a variety of rattan baskets.

The telephone area code is 044. Places to stay include: *Tarin* (ph 514 281, from B550), *New Hotel* (ph 511 341, from B110) and *Memorial* (ph 511 288, from B200).

National Parks

At the end of 1993, there were 77 national parks and wildlife sanctuaries in Thailand, covering $67,366km^2$. This is 13.13% of the total land area. The first park in the country, **Thung Salaeng Luang** was established in 1972. The public have access to national parks but wildlife sanctuaries require permission from the National Parks Division of the Royal Forest Department.

Advance bookings for lodgings and food should be made through the National Parks Division in Bangkok, ph 579 0529. These can be made only one month in advance. *Wildlife Fund Thailand* conduct trips to natural areas and should be contacted; proceeds will go to preserving the country's natural areas.

In North-East Thailand there are several national parks and wildlife sanctuaries near **Loei** and the banks of the **Mekong River**. Cool climate plants, a rare sight in tropical Thailand, can be found at **Phu Kradung National Park**, **Phu Rua National Park** and **Phu Luang Wildlife Sanctuary**.

There are at least 12 marine national parks in Thailand lying in either the Indian or Pacific Oceans. One of the most popular, **Tarutao**, is only 5km from Malaysia's Langkawi Island.

Index of Maps

Captions to Photographs

Facing Inside back cover: Wat Arun at night, Bangkok
Facing 1/2 title page: Dragon Relief, Wat Phra Sing, Chiang Mai
Facing p.16   Lisu girl and Puppets, Mae Sai
Facing P.17   Mud Flats, National Park, Au Nang, Krabi
Facing p.32   Damnoen Saduak Floating Markets
Facing p.33   Traffic Rama IV Road, Bangkok
Facing p.48   Robed Buddha, Wat Phra Mahathat, Ayuthaya
Facing p.49   Thai boy with Kite, Bangkok
Facing p.64   Wat Phra Keo, Bangkok
Facing p.65   Oriental Hotel, Chao Phraya River, Bangkok
Facing p.80   Thai girl, Phimai
Facing p.81   Phra Nang Beach, Krabi
Facing p.176   Markets, Mae Salong
Facing p.177   Northern Thailand looking towards Myanma (Burma)
Facing p.192   High Rise around Patong Beach, Phuket

Index